Politics and the Ghettos

Contributors: | CHARLES R. ADRIAN
ROBERT H. BINSTOCK
JAMES R. DUMPSON
DANIEL J. ELAZAR
TOM HAYDEN
NORTON E. LONG
MELVIN B. MOGULOF
MARTIN REIN
CHARLES I. SCHOTTLAND
ALAN D. WADE
ROLAND L. WARREN
ROBERT C. WOOD
WHITNEY M. YOUNG, JR.

POLITICS
AND THE
GHETTOS

Roland L. Warren, EDITOR

ATHERTON PRESS | New York 1969

Address all inquiries to:
Atherton Press, Inc.
70 Fifth Avenue
New York 10011

Library of Congress Catalog Card Number 77–90771

FIRST EDITION

Manufactured in the United States of America

Designed by Paula Wiener

Foreword

If effective social action is to be taken to eliminate ghetto evils, massive decisions in social policy will be necessary. Such decisions must inevitably take place within the competing kaleidoscopic forces which constitute the political process, broadly conceived.

While the above may seem self-evident, there are few signs that the implications have been drawn from it. Surely one such implication is the need for examining with more clarity and more depth the constellation of political forces within which the ghettos persist as they are today, and for assessing both those political forces which operate to perpetuate the ghetto syndrome and those which operate to change it.

It is therefore a great contribution to make available an interrelated group of papers by experts in various aspects of the relation of politics to the ghettos. These papers were prepared for presentation at the 95th Annual Forum of the National Conference on Social Welfare. Our thanks are due to Roland L. Warren for his leadership in developing these contributions and to the writers for their insightful treatment of a difficult and complex series of topics.

As President of the National Conference during that Forum, I also wish to express my personal thanks to our organizational co-sponsor, the National Assembly for Social Policy and Development.

WAYNE VASEY
School of Social Work
University of Michigan

Contents

CONTRIBUTORS

Charles R. Adrian, Professor and Chairman, Department of Political Science, University of California, Riverside.

Robert H. Binstock, Associate Professor of Politics and Social Welfare, The Florence Heller Graduate School for Advanced Studies in Social Welfare, Brandeis University.

James R. Dumpson, Dean, School of Social Service, Fordham University.

Daniel J. Elazar, Professor, Department of Political Science, and Director, Center for the Study of Federalism, Temple University.

Tom Hayden, Former President, Students for a Democratic Society, Newark.

Norton E. Long, Professor, Department of Political Science, University of Illinois, Urbana; formerly Chairman, Department of Politics, Brandeis University.

Melvin B. Mogulof, Staff Associate, The Urban Institute, Washington, D.C.; formerly Director, Model Cities Program, Department of Housing and Urban Development, Region VI, Los Angeles.

Martin Rein, Professor, Graduate Department of Social Work and Social Research, Bryn Mawr College.

Charles I. Schottland, Dean, The Florence Heller Graduate School for Advanced Studies in Social Welfare, Brandeis University.

Alan D. Wade, Dean, School of Social Work, Sacramento State College.

Roland L. Warren, Professor of Community Theory, The Florence Heller Graduate School for Advanced Studies in Social Welfare, Brandeis University; Chairman of NCSW Division Committee, 1968.

Robert C. Wood, Director, Harvard and Massachusetts Institute of Technology Joint Center for Urban Studies, Cambridge; formerly Undersecretary, Department of Housing and Urban Development, Washington.

Whitney M. Young, Jr., Executive Director, National Urban League, New York City; Past President, National Conference on Social Welfare.

Introduction

In this book thirteen specialists examine the structures and processes of policy-making relevant to the areas of concentrated physical and social deterioration that we now call ghettos. The primary focus of these authors is on the broad policy-making processes that have led to the development of today's ghettos and that, regardless of intent, permit their perpetuation.

An adequate understanding of these processes is a basic precondition for changing them. Such understanding may also help avoid some of the frustration and disappointment stemming from policy programs and proposals that have overlooked the hard realities of political confrontation in a society made up of numerous interest groups, many of them threatened by the changes that are necessary if inroads are to be made on ghetto problems.

The theme of this book is summed up in the title, *Politics and the Ghettos*. This theme does not imply a narrow conception of party politics—although this is certainly included within it—but rather the broader question of how social policy emerges, whether deliberately as the result of conscious attention, or inadvertently as a result of drift and evasion. The procedures that determine policy also include its implementation; we know that policy is formulated not only in legislation and agency policy decisions but also in the process of executive implementation and judicial interpretation.

All the contributors to this volume have addressed themselves to the process of social policy formation specifically regarding the ghettos. The term *ghetto* has been used in much the same sense as that employed by the National Advisory Commission on Civil Disorders: an area within a city characterized by poverty and acute social disorganization, and inhabited by members of a racial or ethnic group under conditions of involuntary segregation.[1] And these contributors deal with social welfare policy in its broadest sense.

The relation between politics and policy is not always clear. English-speaking people are both helped and hindered by the availability of two separate words—*policy* and *politics* —while many languages have only one word for both (French: *politique;* German: *Politik*). The two words permit a distinction between broad guidelines for action and the processes that determine them. But having separated the two, we encounter difficulties in getting them back together—particularly if we purport to be advancing the public interest rather than our own particular interests. In countries that use one word for both, the two ideas—the *what* and the *how*—are fused. In this country we have to make a special effort to fuse them. To neglect the *what* is opportunism. To neglect the *how* is utopianism.

Except for the first chapter, all of the contributions were developed under the auspices of the Division Committee of the National Conference on Social Welfare. Each year the president of that organization appoints a Division Committee with the specific task of developing a coherent series of papers of substantial intellectual content based on a common theme. These papers are then presented as the focus of the extensive program involving hundreds of individual papers and sessions at the annual Forum. Since the theme for the 1968 Forum was "An Action Platform for Human Welfare," the Division Committee found it desirable to choose the allied theme of the relationship between contemporary politics and the ghettos, and to approach this from the different viewpoints represented by the chapter headings of this book.

The reader may be interested in an additional aspect of the development of this volume. The Division Committee arranged to have preliminary drafts of the papers circulated among the members of the Committee as well as among the authors of other papers. A two-day workshop followed, attended by the authors, the Division Committee members, and a small number of invited guests. Here every paper was subjected to the following procedure: It was first reviewed by a predesignated discussant, and then discussed by all present. The author was then free to modify his paper as he saw fit in the light of the discussion, before presenting the final paper at the NCSW Forum in San Francisco. The Russell Sage Foundation contributed a modest amount of money to defray the expenses of this workshop. Whether or not the authors made changes, they and all other participants in the workshop found it an intellectually and emotionally engaging experience. The authors' papers comprise the major part of this book. The opening chapter by the Editor—who was Chairman of the Division Committee—was written after the Forum.

At the San Francisco sessions, each paper except Whitney Young's—which was prepared for a plenary session as the final address of the Forum—was commented on by a discussant (other than the one at the workshop) who had been asked in advance to read the paper critically. These comments were of such high quality that it was decided to include them in this volume. Since many of them were sharply critical of points of view presented in the basic papers, the original authors were invited, in each case, to prepare a brief response. The responses of the authors who accepted this invitation are also included.

The reader will notice many different points of view expressed, some of which are in direct conflict with one another. Obviously, it was not thought desirable to attempt to smooth over these differences in the interest of a speciously attractive consensus. The issues are truly complex and they are subject to diverse interpretations.

Most of the papers are deliberately oriented toward exploring the relations between the existence of the ghetto and the configuration of political forces in various contexts of American society. This strategy, developed by a committee of experts, produced papers which, in one sense, strayed from their objective. These papers largely neglect to trace the configuration of political forces that *sustain* the ghetto, despite the increasing social concern that the ghetto problem raises and despite the heavy, if nevertheless insufficient, social programs which have been developed to combat ghetto conditions. This neglect is pointed out not for purposes of either condemnation or breast-beating, for in the process—almost by serendipity—a number of superb papers were developed, many of them with fresh and intellectually stimulating and even controversial points of view. For such a collection, one need not be apologetic.

Examination of the process by which these papers were deflected from the assignments given to the authors should be instructive. The topic "Politics and Ghetto Perpetuation" was assigned with the intention of developing an examination of the way in which the politics of welfare surrounding the ghettos, whatever the intentions of the actors, results in the ghettos' perpetuation, not their removal. As the last paragraph of the Committee's charge for this paper summarized, "What are the political forces whose net effect is to fail to alter drastically the inequality of opportunity in housing, education, judicial processes, and other areas which lie at the heart of the ghetto problem?"

Norton E. Long developed a brilliant paper taking, at most, only one of the many aspects of this question—the truncated leadership structure of the Negro ghetto community—and drawing from it definite, challenging conclusions regarding black power and black neighborhoods and black city autonomy.

The topic "The Outlook for Creative Federalism" was designed to examine pragmatically the political realities surrounding the type of federal grant-in-aid program that presumably enlists various governmental levels in a creative partnership and that has come to be widely considered as the panacea for the problems of the cities. "What are the political realities underlying creative federalism's promise or lack of promise as an effective mode of resource allocation and multilevel partnership in confronting metropolitan problems generally and ghettos specifically?"

Daniel J. Elazar's treatment of the topic constitutes a masterful and challenging portrayal of an essentially philo-

sophical stance vis-à-vis the question of federalism and the
nature of noncentralized (not decentralized) democracy. In
arguing forcefully for a political philosophy of government
which is both important and controversial, Professor Elazar
has afforded us a significant contribution to political philosophy. But he chose not to direct himself to such matters as
conflicting interest groups, the prior claims made on the
federal budget by the realities of foreign policy and international commitments, the realities of the heterogeneous and
perplexing coalitions that make up the two major political
parties, the special interests of large federal bureaucracies and
their constituencies, the role of national organizations, and
how these and other constraints have operated to limit severely
the possibilities for a federal-state-local partnership in realistically confronting ghetto problems.

Whether or not federal programs aimed at the central
cities should bypass the states or whether the states should
constitute important policymaking and administrative units
in their operation is a much debated question which is highly
relevant to what is made to happen, or not made to happen
—from the standpoint of policy determination—to and within
the ghettos. The charge to the author was laid out in several
paragraphs, all directed toward the concluding question:
"What are the political realities which prevent a more effective state level commitment to the war on poverty and the
ghettos?"

Charles R. Adrian, in his excellent paper, gives a comprehensive resumé of what the states have done that is directly
related to the ghetto problem, and what they might be
expected to do in the future, by way of substantive programs relating to the ghettos. His paper on "The States and
the Ghettos" is directed at the administrative activities of
state governments in various relevant substantive fields. It
forgoes a consideration of the political forces surrounding
and determining the formulation of policy at the state governmental level.

Because of the increasing recognition of the importance
of the systemic linkages between the ghettos and the surrounding metropolitan area—not merely the surrounding city

—it was felt that the metropolitan level should be one of the points of focus in considering the configuration of political forces impacting upon the ghettos. The ghetto is related in systemic ways not only to the surrounding city but to the entire metropolitan community, even though municipal boundaries and governmental forms do not take this into account. The charge to the author is perhaps summarized by the complex sentence which it included: "What are the effects of fragmented jurisdictions, of inadequate taxing powers, of suburban equanimity, of organizations of the poor, especially the black poor, of riots and burnings, of the political machines, of the voluntary agencies and their constituencies, of conflicts in values, of conflicts over land use and social policy—and how do the parts fit together in policy determination?"

The paper by former Under Secretary Robert C. Wood, an eminent political scientist who is an authority on government and politics in metropolitan areas, takes into consideration many relevant aspects of metropolitan-wide politics, but centers on an analysis of what progress has been made and is yet to be made in the solution of ghetto problems. The author reminds us at the outset that he is speaking as a federal official and not as a political scientist, yet his grasp of the historic patterns of change that produced the ghetto, his consideration of the equivocal position of most white suburbanites, and his emphasis on the need for viable metropolitan governmental modes or forms all reveal a scholarly and circumspect approach. Yet he would be the first to admit that he did not address himself in any systematic way to the configuration of political forces within which ghetto policy is made or simply allowed to "drift" within metropolitan areas.

The rationale for inviting an author to develop the topic of "The Ghettos, the New Left and the Revolutionary Ferment" was not that of affording a substantive portrayal of the ideological position of the New Left, or of the programs proposed by various spokesmen for the New Left and the revolutionary ferment, but rather to assess the political importance of this growing phenomenon, otherwise neglected in these papers.

"How are [they] to be assessed as new (in magnitude, at least) elements in the political configuration within which policy gets determined or is allowed to drift and grow? To what extent do they change the configuration of policy-making, and what are their implications for the politics of welfare generally and for the problems of the ghettos, specifically?" It was felt that this paper should be prepared by a representative of the New Left, who could speak with the authority of personal conviction, but who would assess the New Left and the revolutionary ferment as a political force. How would they affect policy, and through what strategies?

Tom Hayden, an obvious choice for this assignment, produced a paper that was received with enthusiastic acclaim at the Forum. Rather than addressing himself directly to the strategy and possible effectiveness of the New Left, he gave a diagnosis of the evils of American society and related this to the model of colonialism, to the growth of black power, to the growth of rebellion, violent and nonviolent, and to possibilities of action by whites who are concerned with the problem. Having thus formulated his paper, he proposed that its title be changed from that of the original charge, "The Ghettos, the New Left, and the Revolutionary Ferment," to "Colonialism and Liberation as American Problems."

The consistent deflection of these papers from their assigned topics as outlined by the Division Committee suggests more than a series of coincidences. Why did the papers consistently avoid the primary focus assigned in each case—the configuration of political forces as these forces affect social welfare policy-making with respect to the ghettos? Several possible explanations suggest themselves:

1. It was both presumptuous and unrealistic to expect such a distinguished group of authors to submit themselves to the detailed constraints imposed by the suggestions of the Committee.

2. Despite repeated attempts to remind the authors of the

nature of the questions which the Committee hoped they would deal with, the authors perceived these as only suggestions, and felt perfectly free to deal with their respective topics precisely as they chose, so long as what they prepared was relevant to their assigned topics.

3. The authors, after reflecting on the matter, decided that the aspects stressed by the Committee were not the most important ones, and decided to treat other features of the political process or even other aspects not directly related to political processes.

4. The authors did not deliberately ignore the charge which was given them, but inadvertently, and naturally, perceived the charge in a manner that warped it in the direction of what they could write most readily and with the least expenditure of effort, or could write with the greatest authoritativeness.

5. In actuality, they could not have been more specific in the treatment of their topics because there are broad gaps in knowledge precisely in the areas indicated by the questions.

My own conclusion regarding these possible explanations is that although any of them may be operative in one or all of the cases, the principal reason for the deflection is the fifth one. We simply do not have a well-developed body of knowledge in this field. We do not yet fully understand nor have we even begun to enumerate and address ourselves systematically to the configurations of political forces at various levels and loci within American society which are primarily determinative in formulating social policy with respect to the ghettos. We have snitches and snatches of knowledge and theory, but nowhere has there been a systematic attempt to bring them together. To do what the Committee hoped would be done, therefore, would not merely have been to reorganize what is already known and apply it to the particular questions raised. It called for a fuller body of facts and a more sophisticated relating of those facts within a theoretical framework than is now available or even readily attainable.

If this is the case, then, this volume's modest success in presenting anything like an adequate systematic analysis of the political configurations of forces determining the politics of welfare in respect to the ghettos constitutes a contribution with greater potential importance than was initially envisaged. It constitutes some of the best analysis that we have available today. And it sets a task for the future.

NOTE

1. *Report of the National Advisory Commission on Civil Disorders* (New York: Bantam Books, 1968), p. 12.

1 | ROLAND L. WARREN

Politics and
the Ghetto System

If the ghettos are not impervious to social intervention techniques, they are at least highly persistent, showing remarkable ability to absorb or ward off attempts at change.

The papers in this volume contain many statements indicating the essential inadequacy of the concerted efforts to date to "do something about" the ghettos, suggesting that much more massive programs must be implemented before basic change can be anticipated. They also point again and again to certain aspects of the ghettos and the situation surrounding them that offer formidable obstacles to the would-be reformer.

One can, of course, find "reasons" for the apparent impermeability of the ghettos and for the relative inadequacy of various efforts to make a marked impact on the configuration of ghetto life. Each point of intervention permits at most a minimal impact which is soon absorbed by the total situation.

Consider some of the apparently futile measures:

Low-cost housing projects, once considered a panacea, have in many instances become dangerous, slovenly, carelessly maintained, and poorly repaired.

In any case, subsidized low-cost housing units in the past three decades have totaled only 800,000, and even the inadequate funds appropriated for them have often not been fully utilized.

An urban renewal program which has as one of its goals "a decent home and a suitable living environment for every American family" has had the net impact of drastically reducing the amount of low-rent housing available to city dwellers.

New school programs designed to upgrade the quality of ghetto schools have been largely unsuccessful, and in any case must confront youngsters who, even as they enter the school, are retarded in their mental development. This retardation increases as they "progress" through the grades.

Job training programs show high dropout rates, and many of those persons who stay with the program are either unable to find work or find it only at menial low-wage occupations.

Welfare programs designed presumably to reduce dependency and to encourage self-sufficient living have the effect of increasing dependency and discouraging self-sufficiency.

Efforts to develop personal, racial, and neighborhood pride in the ghettos and participation in community decision-making are cut back financially and are eventually placed under the control of local municipal authorities.

One could continue giving examples of programs that are either ineffectual or self-defeating, but there is no need to. Several aspects of the problem of the pertinacity of the ghettos are examined in the following papers. None of those papers takes direct occasion to examine the ghetto itself as a tenacious social system, a configuration of mutually supporting circumstances which assures self-perpetuation and whose exchange relationships with the surrounding society are such as, in aggregate, to preserve the system rather than to change it.

The Ghetto as a Social System

It is unwise, as well as unnecessary, to impute to the ghetto as a social system a sort of independent, autonomous existence, deliberately perpetuating itself and fending off all attempts at change. Similarly, it would be tendentious and exaggerated to consider the ghetto simply as the product of a deliberate conspiracy on the part of "the power structure," "white racism," "the establishment," or other reified social phenomena mustered up as scapegoats in a reductionist explanation of a highly complex situation.

There is nevertheless much to support the desirability of looking at the ghetto as a system that perpetuates itself, deliberately or not, and whose relations to the surrounding environment are such as to support and reinforce this self-perpetuation.

To be sure, any social configuration which exists over a period of time can be thought of as a self-perpetuating system, and any such configuration can be shown to be related to larger, more inclusive systems in ways which support it and reinforce it. Yet, many social configurations are nevertheless transitory. Although they may persist for a short or a long time and are reinforced in this persistence through their relationships with their environment, eventually they tend to dissolve. But for the predictable future, the ghettos show little sign of dissolving.

In a sense, the question at issue is what set of circumstances or social policies or events could be expected to dissolve the ghettos rather than perpetuate them, and to dissolve them at a price which is acceptable within the broad scope of American democratic social values. One way of approaching this question is to look at the forces which perpetuate the ghetto configuration. Political processes and social policy, if they are to be relevant to an attack on the ghettos, must confront these forces and overcome them, or at least manipulate them in such fashion as to change the configuration.

A pattern is discernible in the social structure of the ghetto, through which the various parts fit together and reinforce one another. As a convenient outline for examining this pattern we can consider some of the basic social functions which are pertinent to people living in any locality. One such outline is that of five "locality-relevant" functions: Production-distribution-consumption, socialization, social control, social participation, and mutual support.

Production-distribution-consumption is a composite term used to designate the way people get their income and spend it. Ghetto industry is owned to an overwhelming extent by people who do not themselves live in the ghettos. Opportunities for the employment of ghetto dwellers are distributed throughout the city, and even in the suburbs (in the case of domestic help). But there is a high rate of unemployment and the employment available to ghetto dwellers is largely of the unskilled, menial, poorly paid type. Having relatively little experience with the possibilities for long-term saving, or for "rational" budgeting, many ghetto dwellers purchase on impulse and do not use optimally such money as they have. Many, though not all, ghetto stores overcharge the unwary purchaser and often strap him with usurious interest rates for installment purchases. An inordinate proportion of ghetto households are dependent on public assistance payments which bring with them types of agency surveillance which are enervating and degrading.

Socialization refers to the process by which people are trained to become members of society. While the family and the school are considered society's chief instruments for this process, others include churches and other formal institutions, as well as television shows, comic books, and the culture that is communicated by peer groups. The child learns from the people around him, including other children, how to "fit in" and "make a go of things." But what does the Negro ghetto-dwelling child learn? He learns, whether implicitly or explicitly, that he is not quite the equal of other Americans. He learns a way of life that is attuned to squalid and dilapidated living quarters, poor nutrition, an unpleasant experience at school, constant surveillance of his family by society's agents—welfare, probation, school, landlord, police —and he learns to keep his level of aspiration below that of most other Americans. If he wants to be a doctor or a lawyer or an engineer he is quietly and sympathetically counseled to become a medical technologist or a draftsman, or to settle for something less. He is shown daily through word and deed —in school, on the streets, in stores—that he is poor and different from the white majority, and this fact is often transmitted to him by blacks as well.

Social control is a process, vital to all societies, through which members are kept in line with group norms. It may be represented by the formal instruments of the police and courts or the informal constraints on conduct exercised by propaganda, gossip, or social approval and disapproval. It may be imposed from without or, as usually occurs in the process of socialization, may become internalized and speak with the voice of self-discipline or "conscience."

The ghetto dweller is in a special position with regard to the social control processes of the surrounding society. In the first place, the formal processes of social control may work with inordinate rigor on him if he violates one of society's norms. The youngster engaged in mischief in the ghetto is much more likely to be picked up by the police, much more likely to be brought to children's court, much more likely to be packed away to a training school. When he grows older, a similar situation prevails.

But not only the police and the courts are concerned with social control. Many of the institutions which are set up to serve the ghetto dweller turn out to be efforts to control him more than to serve him. Thus, the welfare department, designed to afford him a minimal income when needed, actually engages in exercising various types of control on his conduct. Even the presumably benevolent Police Athletic League or summer camp program may be more explicitly concerned with "preventing delinquency" than with affording the ghetto child a healthy opportunity for recreation. Somehow, the agencies that are supposed to help the ghetto dweller are difficult to enlist in his aid. The public health department can't do much about the rats; the better business bureau can't do much about the exorbitant tenement rents. The ghetto dweller may have to wait in line hours at the clinic; the housing code doesn't seem to ensure that the leaky plumbing is repaired, or that adequate heat is supplied in winter. And the police, presumably there to protect his person and his rights, are at times the most conspicuous violators of both.

Social participation, thought of as membership in and activity in voluntary associations of various kinds, takes on a peculiar form in the ghetto. Various studies indicate a rather live informal network of kinship and friendship. But in terms of organizations that would represent their interests, ghetto residents are underorganized. Such organizations as exist are mostly not indigenous to the neighborhood but rather have been established by others on behalf of the residents. Indigenous organizations, on the other hand, tend, with certain exceptions, to be rather sporadic, often centering around the rise or eclipse of this or that individual leader who succeeds for a time in building an organization through his own personal leadership.

Mutual support, earlier largely a function of the neighborhood and relatives and friends, has come in an urbanized society to be carried on increasingly under formally organized auspices such as social service agencies, hospitals, welfare departments, clinics, and visiting nurse services. We have already noted that such agencies tend in the ghetto to be oriented inordinately toward the function of social control. In addition, the services offered are often extremely poor, and many studies indicate that the ghetto dweller is the object of various forms of discrimination. For example, numerous studies show that both diagnosis and treatment for mental illness are systematically related to the social class of the recipient group. Likewise, the quality of health care has been shown in most studies to be inferior in the case of the ghetto dweller. And, like other agencies and organizations in the ghetto, the agencies of mutual support are typically run by people who do not live there, and who are different in race, in income, and in position in the larger society.

Even this cursory survey of the ghetto as a social system indicates two important points, quite aside from the inferiority of the quality of living conditions offered the ghetto resident. The first is that the ghetto constitutes a system whose parts mutually reinforce one another. As we look across these five locality-relevant functions, we see that they are performed in the ghetto in a manner that virtually assures dependency. Further, they do not train the individual to think of himself as a part of the larger society, but rather to look upon the institutions of the larger society with fear, hostility, and rage.

The other is that the institutions of the ghetto are not those of the ghetto population, but are those of the surrounding society, warped in accordance with the fact they they are "serving" a disadvantaged group, a group for whom the larger values of basic human dignity, justice, and respect for the nobility of each person are somehow less binding.

Seen in this way, the relation of the ghetto to the surrounding society is characterized by reciprocal reinforcement. For on the one hand the public institutions of the ghetto are provided by the surrounding society, and geared to exert controls in the direction of conformity with the larger society, while at the same time providing the "mutual support" dictated by American values. But on the other hand they do so in a manner encouraging dependency, both psychological and economical; discouraging attempts to "break out" into the mainstream; and instilling fear and hatred of the school, the law, and social agencies; thus producing behavior that can be disclaimed with the self-righteous demeanor of people who have "given" much, only to find the recipients "undeserving." In the symbiotic reciprocation between ghetto conditions and the surrounding society, the ghettos constitute a physical locale where disadvantaged people, increasingly blacks, can be segregated from the view of more prosperous and advantaged people in an otherwise affluent society. These disadvantaged people may provide a source of cheap labor, during such times as cheap labor happens to be needed at the margins of economic production; and of course they constitute the occasion for a large and growing industry of social workers and other caretakers and research workers who earn a living above the poverty level by "serving" those below it.

Now of course, like other composites, this composite picture is somewhat imprecise. Not all these disadvantages apply to all black ghetto residents with equal weight. Some ghetto people are employed above the poverty level. Not every experience with the school or with a social service agency or with the welfare department is denigrating. There is an occasional black businessman. Occasionally, the complaint to the code enforcement authority or to the health department is heeded. Not all police are brutal. Not all stores are exploitative. Occasionally, there is an understanding judge. Yet, in the aggregate, the scales tip massively in the indicated direction for black ghetto residents.

This brief sketching out of the perduring systemic aspects of the ghetto configuration has not been given in order to "view with alarm." The point is, rather, to stress that this interrelated system has a great degree of coherence internally and has relationships with other systems in the larger society which make it difficult to change.

Most of the papers in this volume are explicitly concerned not with the internal coherence and pertinacity of the ghetto as a societal form, but rather with the way social policy relevant to the ghetto is developed in the broad confrontation of political forces in American society. One can hardly read these papers without being struck by the specific themes which cut across them, coming up repeatedly in different contexts, and being approached by the authors at times from essentially the same point of view, at times from directly opposite points of view. These themes are important not only because they belong to a diagnosis of the ghetto problem but because they in so many instances imply different types of political action, on which the authors disagree.

Colonialism, Conspiracy, and Collective Guilt

The concept of *colonialism* as an analytical model for understanding social institutions in the ghetto is raised in the paper by Norton E. Long, who asserts with regard to ghetto residents: "Like other colonials, they must learn from their masters the ideology and techniques for their own liberation." Tom Hayden analyzes some of the criticisms that have been made against employing the concept of colonialism with respect to the ghettos, and in turn points out that the criticisms are peripheral and that the basic concept is valid. Robert H. Binstock goes on to point out an essential difference in the colonialism which is based on domination from abroad and that which characterizes American ghettos. In the American case, the "colonials" are not a small dominant minority whose resource base is thousands of miles away, but are a majority with potent resources which would make armed rebellion a carnage.

Whether or not they constitute colonialism, an essential characteristic of ghetto institutions is that they are dominated not by local people, but by others. The people who teach the schools, police the streets, operate the churches, run the social work agencies, provide health services, own the stores, run the industry, and fight the fires are not ghetto people; the organizations that employ them are not run by ghetto people; and the policies they follow are not set by ghetto people. Rather, whether one thinks of them as helpers or exploiters, they represent the functionaries in a process over which ghetto people have little control and with which they feel little sense of identification. In this sense, ghetto institutions are similar to those of an occupying power, and in this sense a diagnosis of the politics of welfare must address itself to the forms in which valid local representation may be attained, and how these forms can be achieved.

A second *theme*, which is only occasionally in the fore-front of attention in these papers but lurks ubiquitously in the background, is perhaps best conveyed by the word *conspiracy*. The conspiracy theme relates to two orders of phenomena, one involving the dominant society surrounding the ghetto and the other involving ghetto residents themselves. It is perhaps best introduced by alluding to the consideration of the ghetto as a coherent social system which was presented on p. 12. One can approach the "conspiracy" issue by considering the proposition: *If it had been the conscious intent of white society to produce a subsystem within American society in which Negroes would be segregated and within which they would be controlled, exploited, and continually forced into a position of second-class citizenship, both in their own perception and in that of whites, such an intention could not have been fulfilled more effectively than by developing the present system of black ghettos.*

This proposition implies that the system works so well that it can hardly be by chance. It is, whether directly or indirectly, the solution of a white society of Judeo-Christian traditions to the problem of how to keep blacks in subjection while still maintaining an alleged loyalty to the ideal values. Hence, the police brutality, the failure to enforce housing codes, the shoddy treatment given welfare recipients, the physical neglect of street cleaning and ghetto public facilities, the failure to activate an adequate housing program, and so on, are not merely a series of coincidental "problems," failures to implement the American dream in a number of isolated cases. They are rather the result of a systematic policy, partly conscious, partly unconscious, of subjugation of black people by white people. This, it would seem, is the underlying rationale of the charges of white racism, and of the recent ascendancy of that term over the term that was much more common until fairly recently—racial discrimination.

The aggregate result, in other words, appears so purposeful and so coherent that the assumption of purposeful, deliberate collective intent seems the only logical one. The ghetto configuration works *as if* white society were definitely wanting it that way and consciously planning it that way. Hence, the "plot," or "conspiracy."

The issue seems unresolvable on this level of analysis, since different people may contemplate the same set of interconnected data and some will call them a conspiracy and others will not. The approach from social system theory is helpful for purposes of understanding what is involved. One of the principal concerns of general systems theory, for example, is the recognition that various systems function as though they had a purpose. Whether or not they can be called purposeful without imputing some kind of "conscious" purposefulness is a much debated issue, which even extends to cybernetic systems.[1] The "invisible hand" which Adam Smith saw guiding the market process illustrates another aspect of the phenomenon. Systems act in ways which, when observed, seem to imply purposive, aggregate, centralized direction, even where it can be readily demonstrated that such direction does not take place.

The point is somewhat more readily understood when Merton's distinction between manifest and latent functions is taken into account. Put most simply, Merton recognized

that certain behaviors may have the explicit purpose of accomplishing goal *A*, but quite apart from this may also
operate in such a matter as to bring about the accomplishment of goal *B*, even when goal *B* was not consciously a
part of the planning.[2]

To say this is not to establish that in the case of white
racism there is no conspiracy, but rather merely to point out
that the conspiracy issue cannot be demonstrated simply by
pointing to the circumstance that any given system functions "as if" there were conscious, deliberate purpose and
controlled direction to the total system.

Interestingly, the issue is dramatized by the attitudes of
various parties on the matter of "collective guilt" for white
racism. For example, the National Advisory Commission on
Civil Disorders concluded: "What white Americans have
never fully understood—but what the Negro can never forget
—is that white society is deeply implicated in ·the ghetto.
White institutions created it, white institutions maintain it,
and white society condones it."[3] Hubert H. Humphrey, who
was Vice President at the time, stated in a prepared address:
"The contention by the President's riot commission that white
society condones negro slums comes dangerously close to
a doctrine of group guilt."[4]

In relation to the "conspiracy" question, this concept of
group guilt could lead to an interesting and lengthy digres-
sion. Let us permit ourselves only a brief one. Modern social
philosophy does not quite countenance the justice of the
Old Testament God in punishing the Egyptians for the mis-
deeds of their Pharaoh, for which they were not individually
guilty. Likewise, there are many people who still remember
with consternation the destruction of the entire community
of Lidice, Czechoslovakia, by the Nazis in retribution for the
slaying of a Gestapo leader there. Christianity, by and large,
modified the doctrine of collective guilt or collective salva-
tion, for that matter, and in effect placed both on a more
individual basis, so that in this sense, at least, *Pilgrim's Progress* is the Christian counterpart of the book of Exodus.
Despite the values which have been ascribed to this more
individualized viewpoint, in which the matter of guilt or inno-

cence came to be laid on the individual rather than the group and in which motivation, purity of heart, and questions of individual intent became uppermost, there appears today to be a growing body of thought which indicates that this individualization of moral responsibility involves a high price, particularly in complex societies where individuals are inextricably bound up in systemic networks whose aggregate effect may be largely unrelated to individual motivation and individual morality. The point has been well developed by Reinhold Niebuhr in his *Moral Man and Immoral Society*.[5] The relevance of the question for the ghettos is indicated by the perplexity with which many white middle class "liberals" consider their own relationship to the ghetto problem and "white racism." They feel that in their own personal lives they have tried to free themselves from prejudice, have "given to worthy causes" on behalf of the Negro, have defended racial equality in country club locker rooms and civic associations to the point of infuriating their less enlightened friends, have gone out of their way to associate with Negroes on a basis of equality. They have voted for the political leader who seemed to be the most genuinely concerned about racial justice.

Yes, they live in a white suburb, while the black ghettos fester, but they have been trying for years to promote open housing in their own community. Yes, they earn their living from a company which has inordinately few Negro employees in the white collar brackets, and so on through the school, the church, social activities, and government; but they wish things were different.

Yet, earnest though they may be, they recognize that in all these cases they are participating in and benefiting from institutions that, despite their own wishes, are, in their totality, racist—at least in the sense that in their aggregate outcome they produce the various conditions described as racial injustice. Herein lies what appears to be valid in the issue of white racism and collective guilt.

Unfortunately, we do not have a social ethic which accommodates adequately the type of conceptual analysis and empirical finding which arise from a social system approach

to the ghettos. We are left either with a stupendous aggregate evil, but no individual evildoers; or, taking the other
horn of the dilemma, we are asked to feel individually guilty
for circumstances over which we have no individual control.
Meanwhile, the exploitative system persists and awaits an
ethic which can adequately handle the individual's relationship to large, impersonal systems.

The other relevant aspect of the "conspiracy" question has
been widely debated—the sense in which ghetto rioting and
arson can be considered on the one hand to be merely a
blind, visceral type of lashing out, a catharsis through rage—
and the sense in which it can be considered as purposeful,
goal oriented, a deliberate means of "telling Whitey how
things are going to be." The National Advisory Commission
on Civil Disorders was quite explicit about the widespread
riots of 1967:

"On the basis of all the information collected the Commission concludes that the urban disorders of the summer
of 1967 were not caused by, nor were they the consequence
of, any organized plan or 'conspiracy.' "[6]

Yet, whether or not organized, many aspects of the rioting,
particularly of the arson and looting, appeared to be purposive, as did the similar activity after the assassination of
Dr. Martin Luther King, Jr. The distinction here is not
whether the riots performed a (latent) function, but whether
that function was significant in the motivation of the actors.
The evidence to support the latter seems to be meager, at
least for the vast majority of participants.

Neighborhood Autonomy, Black Power, and the Revolutionary Ferment

A recurrent theme in the papers is that of *neighborhood
autonomy*. It is perhaps best approached through the consideration of a point already raised: that the institutions of
the ghetto, whether or not they are (manifestly) *for* ghetto
residents, are not *by* them. Both Tom Hayden and Norton
E. Long emphasize the great importance of neighborhood
autonomy, and Daniel J. Elazar asserts that neighborhood

autonomy, far from being opposed to a "creative federalism," is actually one of its preconditions. As Elazar points out, there has been a turnabout in which the "progressives," or "liberals," who for the past three decades have been advocating the centralization of decision-making into more and more inclusive units, especially the federal government, are now decrying the curse of bigness in bureaucracies, the essential oppression of the mass society, and are advocating participatory democracy on a decentralized basis, including neighborhood autonomy. More specifically, black leaders and white liberals are stressing the necessity of neighborhood autonomy in the ghettos, the necessity for ghetto people to control the institutions that influence their lives in their own neighborhoods.

The current zig-zagging course of the neighborhood autonomy issue is hardly unprecedented. The "neighborhood unit" as an important basis for association in addition to a mere aggregation of dwellings and facilities emerged several decades ago. The concept, expounded and promoted by Clarence Arthur Perry,[7] achieved wide popularity in subsequent decades among architects and city planners. But the idea of making much of the neighborhood as a *social* unit was attacked as largely anachronistic and irrelevant by planners such as Reginald Isaacs[8] and sociologists such as Richard Dewey.[9] During this same period, there was a great proliferation of neighborhood or community council organizations, neighborhood centers, Alinsky-type organizations, and other types of social arrangement designed to promote the values inherent in the neighborhood, which was perceived as a social unit under threat of engulfment by the institutions of mass society. Gradually, however, there grew the realization that the major institutions which control the lives of people in their neighborhoods are not controlled by those neighborhoods, either in the ghettos or elsewhere.

Now that the wheel has again turned, and the concern for neighborhood autonomy is being voiced loud and strong by or on behalf of ghetto residents, there remains the basic question as to how relevant the neighborhood is as a unit of social organization in a period when so many vital decisions and policies affecting neighborhood living are made at the city-wide level or the state level, or, with increasing volume, at the national level. Putting this question in sharpened form: If Scarsdale cannot be autonomous, can Harlem? If Winchester cannot be autonomous, can Roxbury? If Grosse Point cannot be autonomous, can inner Detroit?

Yet, though underlining the issue, such questions do not help clarify it. Rather, the question is *what* types of power over *what* types of behavior or public or private facility are relevant for decentralization to the neighborhood level, and what types of transfers and transformations do these involve? A consideration of some fairly widespread demands of black power advocates indicates that there remain many highly relevant issues: control over decentralized functions of local government, such as police, sanitation, public welfare, health, and other facilities, by local ghetto residents; similar control over schools, devolvement of ownership of present ghetto business establishments to ghetto residents, and development of new, locally owned enterprises; encouragement of entrepreneurship by indigenous residents; reversal of the development toward city-wide "at large" election of council members, so as to move toward election by wards or districts—and, in general, substantial control by neighborhood residents over activities designed to serve ghetto people.

Certainly, these issues are relevant to the neighborhood level, and are somewhat different, though perhaps more pertinent, than those associated with earlier, well-meaning efforts toward "neighborhood improvement" endeavors. Yet, these issues exist only within the parameters of still larger issues: How much income is accessible to neighborhood residents through national and state public assistance or alternative income maintenance programs? How much money is available to neighborhood schools through federal and state funding? What kinds of loans for mortgages, business investment, and other purposes are available through the federal government? How much in federal or state funds comes into the municipal treasury and is thus available for the development and improvement of municipal services and facilities in the neighborhood? How much is available for low-cost housing? These are questions that are not immediately approachable through neighborhood organizations, and past attempts to coordinate neighborhood organizations across the country on behalf of social policies affecting *all* neighborhoods have usually been both miniscule and ineffective.

Closely related to the theme of neighborhood autonomy has been that of *black power*. There is obviously wide divegence between the views of Norton E. Long and those of Robert C. Wood. It would be gratuitous to seek here to add to the heated, many-sided literature on the subject of black power—except to note one related item, highly conspicuous by its omission from the papers included in this volume: the fact that the majority of the poor in the United States are white, and the implication of this for an evaluation of equating ghettos with blackness and neighborhood autonomy in the ghettos with black power.

Four aspects of this circumstance merit consideration here. First is the importance of the fact that the war on poverty and the more recent Model Cities program have come increasingly to be thought of, by blacks and whites alike, as programs for blacks. This development, needless to say, has had both positive and negative repercussions among various parts of the white population.

But second, the outcome has been that the poor white, whether in the city ghetto or in disadvantaged rural areas, has been underrepresented both numerically and—perhaps more important—symbolically in the decision-making both by the poor and by the nonpoor as regards measures presumably to benefit the poor.

Third, the comparative neglect of the white poor both numerically and symbolically can but serve to strengthen a bitter and ironic aspect of the entire race/poverty configuration: that often, the bitterest enemy of the poor black is the poor white.

Fourth, the issue as stated by Norton E. Long, though clear, is somewhat oversimplified. It is not a question of black cities for black people. It is rather a question of the mixture of control of various groups, minorities and majorities, which remains whether the majority in a particular city, or city neighborhood, is black or white. Should a city whose voters are 51 percent black have 100 percent black control, and a city which is 51 percent white have 100 percent white control? Despite the prevalence of segregational practices aimed at blacks, the ghettos—by any set of objective criteria of poverty of residents, dilapidation of housing, or disadvantaged circumstances in other aspects of social organization —are far from exclusively black. People with experience in the competition among ethnic groups—blacks, Puerto Ricans, whites (including national-origin groups), Mexican-Americans—know that the ghetto problem cannot be approached realistically in terms of all-or-none Blackism. The relations between a black majority and a white minority of heterogeneous composition present an agenda concerning which many alternatives are possible—including the continuation of the oppression of minority groups, only this time by blacks.

A final theme, which constituted part of the prescribed topic for Tom Hayden's paper, is the *revolutionary ferment*. It was felt necessary or at least desirable to single out the topic of the New Left and the "revolutionary ferment" for special treatment as an emerging force in policy determination processes with respect to the ghettos. Conceivably, one would have found repeated allusion to it in most of the other papers, and indeed this might have been the case if the authors had not known that it was to receive intensive treatment in a separate paper.

Taken as a whole, the net impact of these papers would seem to indicate the essential conservatism of the existing channels through which social policy regarding the ghettos is formulated in the American political process. As Alan D. Wade indicates, the process of decision-making around welfare politics at the federal level as depicted in Charles I. Schottland's comprehensive analysis is essentially conservative and elitist. On balance, one is justified in entertaining doubts as to whether a great amount of impetus for change is to be expected from this source, or from the forces around the various State Houses of the nation, or from the complex metropolitan configurations of which the ghettos are an integral—and necessary—part.

Where, then, would be the new dynamic forces that could begin to alter the configuration of decision-making to such an extent that the most-needed changes will actually take place?

Perhaps the greatest dynamic is from the ghetto itself. For something is stirring there. One can think of this something in terms of four interrelated components. There is the growing process of organization of the poor to speak for their own interests, rather than being spoken for by the nonpoor. There are the riots, which dramatize the stirring of a mighty and potentially cataclysmic force capable of tearing the cities apart. There is black power, the increasing realization on the part of Negroes that they will not be given their share of the benefits of a highly productive society but will have to struggle for them as Negroes. And there is the growing surge toward decentralization, a surge which goes far beyond the question of whether this or that school system or this or that municipal service will be decentralized, and constitutes by now the proportions of a social movement.

Underlying all these, there is the revolutionary ferment—the noise from the streets, the daily-accumulating new ways of seeking to influence the decision-making process by other than conventionally sanctioned means. The ghettos are caught up in this revolutionary ferment, being, among other things, part of the symbols and part of the substance of a social order whose basic premises are undergoing critical scrutiny. This questioning of the fundamental principles of our society is occasioned because of both the gap between ideal values and social reality, and increasing skepticism as to whether the ideal values, themselves, are valid. But the ghettos are only part of the subject-matter of the rebellion. "Mass society" is also indicted. So is centralized power. So is American society's overelaboration of its material culture. Conventional methods for carrying on policy contest—the political debate, the ballot, the educational campaign, the political pressure group, the letter to the editor, the legal contest—are themselves under indictment as being patently inadequate to effect the changes that are indispensable if injustices such as those of the ghettos are to be eliminated.

As these words are being written, the hot summer of 1968 is coming upon us, the Poor People's March is taking place in Washington, and the President of the United States has acceded to Congressional demands for a 6 billion dollar budget cut. The implication is clear to thousands of Americans: the conventional channels of public policy formation in the United States are incapable of confronting the crisis unless they are constantly being pressed by the "noise from the streets." Even among the thousands who take recourse to norm-violating methods of social policy participation—the draft-card burners, the students who seize control of universities, the ghetto rioters, the peace vigilers, the armed black militants—there are many who prefer that the established system for policy-making not adapt itself to the pressure from the streets but instead be destroyed, to be replaced by an allegedly more equitable one.

Can the system right what an increasing number of people are coming to consider to be its tragic wrongs—both at home and abroad—before it disintegrates under the twin pressures of external rebellion and internal anomic immobilization? Or will it be destroyed? Or do we confront the prospect of still another century of exploitation and racial injustice?

These, it would appear, are the basic questions which underlie the politics of welfare today. In seeing this, the New Left raises the right questions, whether or not it supplies the right answers. (As a matter of fact, it supplies precious few answers, good or bad, which even attempt to present clear and viable alternatives to the status quo.)

As one black civil rights leader put it, "We must try to prevent riots like we had last summer but if they occur, we can't afford to waste them." He is not a militant. Quite the opposite. But he catches, in this statement, the sense that if the political system is to face up to its huge problems, it will need plenty of "push" from the outside. Here, the "outside" means all the unconventional methods of social policy participation that help make this an exciting and fateful era.

The forces at work are truly revolutionary. It would be foolish to take for granted that the changes they produce will occur peacefully.

NOTES

1. Cf. Walter Buckley, ed., *Modern Systems Research for the Behavioral Scientist: A Sourcebook* (Chicago: Aldine, 1968), especially Part V, Section A: "Cybernetics and Purpose."
2. Robert K. Merton, *Social Theory and Social Structure,* rev. ed. (New York: The Free Press of Glencoe, 1957), pp. 19ff.
3. *Report of the National Advisory Commission on Civil Disorders* (New York: Bantam, 1968), p. 2.
4. *The New York Times,* March 25, 1968.
5. Reinhold Niebuhr, *Moral Man and Immoral Society: A Study in Ethics and Politics* (New York: Scribner's, 1932).
6. *Report of the National Advisory Commission on Civil Disorders,* p. 202.
7. Clarence Arthur Perry, *The Neighborhood Unit,* Monograph I of Vol. 7, *Regional Survey of New York and Its Environs,* Committee on Regional Planning of New York, 1929.
8. Reginald Isaacs, "Are Urban Neighborhoods Possible?" *Journal of Housing* (July 1948).
9. Richard Dewey, "The Neighborhood, Urban Ecology, and City Planners," *American Sociological Review,* 15:4 (August 1950).

2 | NORTON E. LONG

Politics and
Ghetto Perpetuation

As Herbert Hill maintains, "The meaning of the term 'ghetto' has significantly changed since the 1920s when Louis Wirth and other sociologists used the word to describe a voluntary community of ethnic group concentration. Now it refers to an area of socially and economically deprived people belonging to a racial caste group suffering acute social disorganization and enforced segregation. The current residents of the ghetto remain outside the 'opportunity structure' of the larger society."[1] Hill's definition is a useful point of departure; it points to some of the salient differences between the contemporary American "ghetto" and earlier segregated enclaves in larger societies.

The existence of separate, segregated groups in cities carrying on a life of exchange, but highly restricted social contact, with other groups and the larger society is a frequent occurence in history. The term "quarter" is familiar and of long standing. Segregation as a mutual adaptation to cultural and religious difference had little invidiousness for those assured of their own identity and its worth. A commercial relationship has the universalism of trade, carrying with it its own presumption of a limited equality in the mutual advantage of free exchange. The characteristic of the pluralism of the city of the past was the quasi self-governing nature of the ethnic commercial enclave. It was alien and self-governing to an important degree.

The Chinatown of nineteenth-century San Francisco was segregated by external and internal desire. While it did not have a status like the Western treaty ports, its ruling elders had the benevolent acceptance of their authority by the larger society. The ethnic enclave had to all intents and purposes a government of its own and hence a social structure. To be sure, this government and social structure was the product of its folk culture and social technology. It did not have to be invented and it was not destroyed.

Slavery in the American South systematically destroyed social structure, even reaching to the family itself. The master class carefully saw to it that its slaves were deprived of a social structure that might have provided leadership and organization for resistance. Even literacy in a preindustrial system could be forbidden to a plantation work force. With the destruction of the Freedman's Bureau the post-Civil War attempt to counteract the effects of slavery was abandoned and a new system of enforced servility was established. This system involved the occupation of all the formal posts of social control by whites and the condemnation of successful Negroes to social isolation or, more frequently, to the function of white tools for the readier maintenance of their fellows' subordination.

In effect, Negroes had, instead of their own social control structure, a white hierarchy assisted by collaborationists of their own kind. The social system to which they were socialized in the South was one in which social control was alien and their own upper class was on the white payroll or withdrawn. This pattern produced a system where the only indigenous culture was lower class—the only culture the mass of people could have confidence in as their own. It also produced a socialized pattern of distrust of leaders, a highly deserved one given graphic portrayal in Ralph Ellison's *Invisible Man*. It also produced a leadership style that would reinforce that distrust.

Ghetto Leadership Structure

Kenneth Clark's *Dark Ghetto* gives poignant expression to the dominance of the ghetto by lower class culture and life style. It vividly describes the intractable problem of creating stable, effective leadership in a corrosive atmosphere of mutual distrust, anarchic individualism and opportunism.[2] James Wilson's study of "Negro Politics" is subtitled "The Search for Leadership." Wilson is less pessimistic than Clark about the possibilities of this development. However, his details on the incapacity of a Negro population of nearly a million to produce more than a pittance for such institutions as the Provident Hospital in Chicago is a grim measure of its social incapacity to mobilize resources.[3] Thus far, even militant groups have been heavily dependent on white contributions. The Negro middle class until recently has been escapist, seeking to flee the constant threat of being swallowed into the poverty-stricken mass from which it has emerged. Its strategy where it cannot physically flee has been to seek a physical coexistence with a spiritual isolation.

The outstanding fact is that middle class Negroes do not govern the ghetto. They are afraid of it and they would escape it if the walls of prejudice would permit. The governing class of the ghetto is white, from police, social work, schools, business, on up. The muddle over Negro identity has made this situation seem natural and transitory. Negroes, like French colonials, were supposed to be in the process of complete assimilation when skin colors would make no difference for role assignment.

But assimilationist theory has failed. Indeed it has obscured the need for a Negro role structure duplicating the white if the servile past were to be overcome. A stratified social structure with Negroes at the bottom was built into a system where Negroes were governed by whites with their own middle class alienated and escapist. An alien white middle class could not dominate the value structure of the ghetto. The price of a Negro middle class that did not govern has been the dominance of the ghetto by lower class Negro culture, the only authentic culture it has.

The disorganizing effect of this combination of white middle class occupation of the social control roles and lower class Negro culture providing the only authentic indigenous values has been extreme. It is not surprising that Negro militants preach a doctrine that sounds both revolutionary and bourgeois, combining puritanism, Horatio Alger, and Frantz Fanon. From the point of view of the maintenance of white dominance, the disorganizing dominance of Negro lower class culture is highly functional. However, its costs in the destruction of the conditions needed for the creation of a productive labor force, its reinforcement of dependency, and its tendency to create sullen apathy punctuated by violence are very great. The post-slavery adaptation is difficult to break. Negroes, unlike other ethnics, are unequipped with a political and social technology from a pre-American past which they can adapt to the solution of their problems. Like other colonials, they must learn from their masters the ideology and techniques for their own liberation. Indeed they must be goaded by some of their masters into producing leaders of their own. As Glazer and Moynihan point out, the Negro's problem is that, being wholly an American, he has no past with which to fashion a different present.[4] Being wholly an American, he has only lately come to realize his utter need of an ethnic identity of his own.

Earlier ethnics were frequently cut off from their own middle and upper classes by migration. Not until the communist take-over did many American cities learn that there were educated Poles, Hungarians, or Yugoslavs. But the lower class character of the migration did not mean, despite crudities and vulgarities, that the migrants did not carry with them a model of an appropriate role structure that they would seek to reproduce. They came from civilization, not plantation slavery or serfdom. The Chinese coolie that helped build the railways was illiterate and unskilled, but in one most important way he was both literate and skilled; he was heir to a social technology which he could replicate rather than have to invent. While the ethnic enclaves of our cities have not been formally self-governing, they have been socially organized. This has meant that they have been systems of social cooperation.

As Glazer and Moynihan point out, the Chinese produced restaurants and laundries as a niche for themselves in the economy and helped each other in doing so. Jews, Irish, Italians, and Poles developed small businesses and broke from the ethnic economy into the larger economy. Employment of fellow ethnics by contractors has been a major device in overcoming union barriers to new entrants to the construction trades. The costs of a purely lower class culture of immediate consumption have been a failure to make use of economic avenues of upward mobility that others have used to good purpose. The lack of Negro middle class power in the ghetto has meant that its not inconsiderable resources have been dissipated rather than mobilized as social capital.

Skin color and discrimination are frequently cited as the major barriers that prevent Negroes emulating the career of other ethnics. The recent experience of the Chinese and Japanese casts doubt on this explanation. Dorothy Newman points out:

The status of the Chinese and Japanese in 1930 was probably lower, in terms of occupational pattern, than that of Negroes in 1960. Economic as well as social prejudice against Chinese and Japanese was very strong, particularly on the West Coast (where even today Oriental Americans are concentrated).

By 1950, however, the Chinese and Japanese showed almost twice as large a proportion as Negroes in professional, managerial (including farming), and clerical occupations, and, correspondingly, a much smaller proportion in crafts or production work in industry. . . .

By 1960, the Chinese and Japanese had outstripped the white population in the degree of concentration in professional and technical occupations and in the white-collar occupation groups as a whole.[5]

This experience pretty well shows that despite prejudice and discrimination, groups that can effectively utilize education can achieve upward mobility in the occupation structure in an expanding economy.

Blau and Duncan's study of the American occupational structure makes clear that upward mobility is still a major feature of the American economy. However, while their study does show a lessening of discrimination at the unskilled levels, it also shows a disheartening increase of discrimination as it affects educated Negroes.[6] Herman Miller in his *Rich Man, Poor Man* shows that at every occupational level Negroes get less than whites and that white-nonwhite income differentials are not narrowing.[7] How much of this is due to prejudice and how much to the inferior quality of education given to Negroes and to factors affecting Negroes' ability to make use of what education there is available is an interesting question. Miller, who is certainly a sympathetic witness, cites the experience under civil service and particularly that of the Library of Congress where Quincy Mumford, the Librarian, was devoted to equal employment opportunity.

The very low proportion of Negroes in the top-grade jobs is attributed by Mumford to "the minimum of qualified Negro applicants."[8] Charles Silberman, also a sympathetic witness, points to an array of high status opportunities which, despite the general discrimination, are going begging for lack of qualified applicants.[9]

Perhaps the Japanese and Chinese ability to overcome discrimination and "make it" in a world of civil service and business tests merely highlights the Negro's problem. His problem may be more than discrimination and prejudice—a condition in which he lacks resources of his own comparable to theirs to use education as a means to surmount the barriers of a white civil service world even where, as in government, that civil service may be formally fair and open. It may be that a Negro middle class will have to be brought into being by means other than through the present slow process of upward mobility insured by an ineffective and ineffectively used educational system. The civil service that ethnics fought for to remove the patronage grip of the Irish and the machine might be a costly luxury if it removes jobs and positions of social control from the reach of the Negroes. Quite conceivably we may have better-run cities with formally poorly qualified patronage-appointed Negroes serving as teachers, policemen, firemen, and even as supervisors, than by better-qualified whites. This might prove the case because Negroes might better respond to their own. Even more, public employment in the control positions of their society may be necessary to create and staff a disciplined Negro social structure. The technology and habit of self-government are quite possibly essential for an ethnic group to be able to cooperate, maintain a normative structure, and utilize institutions such as schools. If this is so, a degree of self-government is requisite to a social structure, self-respect, and capacity for self-help.

Actually the drift course of events is leading this way. The disenchantment of Negro militants with the results of the Civil Rights campaign has led to "black power." While this slogan has alarmed many with the fear that prolonged white instruction has finally produced a complementary Negro racism, it is most generally given definition as a demand for a respected and respectable Negro identity and an appropriate degree of Negro self-determination. This has occasioned some psychological and actual unemployment of whites who have been urged to do their missionary work among whites. It has had the wholly healthy result of Negroes recognizing that a Negro cause must be led by Negroes. Conceivably it might lead to Negroes being able to break their debilitating dependence on white financing. While the integrationists who are also assimilationist deplore the Negro attempt to secure a separate identity and self-determination, they might discover that this is a necessary prelude to mutual self-respect in a pluralist society. In a world in which the nation-state seemed a dangerous anachronism the creation of the state of Israel and other new states might seem a sheer atavism, but who has the alternative for skipping this stage and who can deny latecomers what they themselves have long enjoyed?

Black power is a demand for black identity and self-determination. Its expression ranges from fantasies of a revolutionary take-over of power from the whites, possibly worldwide; or the creation of a separate state; to sober, entirely possible though difficult, possibilities of black governments within the larger society and black participation in the government of the larger society. Since the communists proposed a black republic in the thirties, it has been fashionable to regard the decolonialization model and the notion of separatism as a piece of romanticism or demagogy. In the form then presented and in some of the forms now suggested, the conception is romantic or demogogic. But a species of communal politics with considerable degree of autonomy has been possible in a variety of societies ranging from India to the United States. What might be new would be the dependence of whites on the tender mercies of nonwhites for a change.

It is certainly true that Negroes have suffered from being an economy within an economy. However, it is by no means absurd for Negroes to follow the path of other ethnics in creating their own businesses, exploiting their own market, and attempting to break into the larger economy. Some such strategy has been helpful for others including, despite the teachings of classical economics, new countries. The fact that most large businesses will be white owned and white controlled does place limits on any Negro apartheid. It also creates problems for a black power leadership that must at once maintain its credibility as authentic black leaders rather than Uncle Toms. White dominance over national business enhances the importance of local Negro business and the local public sector for autonomous Negro leadership roles. This is not wholly dissimilar to the problem of autonomous leadership in any community whose economic life is dominated by national corporations. Some of the literature indicates that branch plant managers of national corporations have been content—more than content—to confine themselves to public relations and defensive tactics. Local government has been left to locals.

White Flight and Black Control

The drift course of American life is toward the creation of conditions appropriate for black power—Negro government in some and perhaps many of our cities. The massive white exodus to the suburbs engendered by life style but enhanced by racial fears may be further accelerated by riots and crime in the streets. The liberal policy of integration which may have served upper income Negroes but has delayed effective action to house low income Negroes shows signs of wearing thin and may be abandoned. Frances Piven and Richard Cloward argue in the December 1966 *New Republic* that insistence on racial integration has weakened support for housing programs at the expense of the poor. A policy of "either integrated housing or no housing" has meant inaction. In a recent issue of *Dissent* Chester Hartman says, "Depressing as it may be to white liberals, the truth must be faced: to insist upon racial integration as a *sine qua non* of housing improvement is to consign millions of American families, white and black, to their present slum conditions for years to come." Herbert Hill has documented the increasing segregation of American life as Negro migration to the central city and Negro fertility accompanied by white flight.[10] The condition is massive and probably for some time irreversible.

White flight as Bernard Frieden shows is not for Negroes an unmixed evil.[11] Indeed it is the overwhelming means by which Negroes improve their housing condition. Given the income levels of Negroes both now and in the near future it seems that for them housing will be upgraded mainly by a process of transfer and upgrading of the existing stock. Whites who are attached to central cities and older suburbs view this process with alarm and fear. In the smaller aging suburb it can move with forest-fire rapidity. Thus East Cleveland was 2.4 percent nonwhite in 1960. Today 50 percent of its school population is nonwhite. As in neighborhood transition one of the appalling costs is the price in deferred maintenance and waste of social capital entailed by a period of uncertainty and drift. Whites may abandon schools long before they abandon political control of the city. With their own children elsewhere and with declining tax bases they may hold down school expenditures. School personnel, faced with a grim future, pull out and the school system as a going concern deteriorates. What happens to the schools may happen to the other social institutional capital.

The problem of the city in transition is not unlike the problem of colonial transition. The rulers are leaving. The ruled have not been taught or given experience in ruling.

There is justifiable fear of what this lack of competence may mean even without counting the hatreds and resentments that may surface. Again like a colonial situation the white rulers own valuable properties with sunk costs in the cities in transition. Unlike white ethnics some businessmen and many enlightened corporation executives are not appalled by a black-governed city. What they are appalled by is the fact that an impoverished, politically inexperienced black community may hold their property to ransom. Despite the protection of the courts, possibly even of state legislatures, property might be in serious jeopardy. Past attempts at the white recolonization of the city are not only due to the aspiration of white politicians to insure their political futures but of white businessmen to insure their properties. The elections in Gary and Cleveland showed that while it is possible for some businessmen as in Cleveland to attempt the role of statesmen, the overwhelming majority of white ethnics will join the resistance.[12] It is somewhat doubtful that the "white power structure" will be able or wish to restrain and direct rather than ride with the forces that applaud Governor Wallace and use crime in the streets as a euphemism for Negro protest.

The natural thrust of white flight and Negro concentration in central cities and older suburbs is to create the preconditions for Negro governments and black power. At its best this could create the opportunity for Negroes to lose their sense of powerlessness and with self-government develop a social structure that might provide a prideful identity and the capacity to work together and make effective use of institutions such as schools. There is no reason to believe such a result would be easy or automatic. One might expect an array of Negro governments that at their worst might range from the Haiti of Papa Dor to the Congo. The fact that such a range has sometimes characterized white local governments will not reduce the demand for the Marines where whites are involved.

The key question is whether there exists and can rapidly be produced sufficient middle class cadres to govern a black governed city. White ethnics might loathe the menace of such a city to their ethnic pride. Who would now be at the bottom? But white businessmen might find it an attractive if secure place to do and even to conduct business. A black-governed city might turn an alienated, sullen, and incompetent under-class into a valuable addition to the labor force. Other whites might find a black-governed city, once it got over its Baptist *cum* Muslim puritanism, a welcome addition to the meager variety of American life. The great fear is clearly that the middle class Negroes, as Kenneth Clark suggests, cannot dominate the lower class culture of ghetto life. The fate of the Barbadians mentioned by Glazer and Moynihan is a case in point. This ethnic group possessed all the promising middle class aptitudes and habits but are now completely submerged in lower class Negro New York.[13]

The major argument for integration is that the Negro middle class needs it to survive and that only the white middle class is strong enough to shape up the Negro lower class. If this is accepted it leads to the conclusion that the ghetto as an intergenerationally sustained culture of poverty and social disorganization must be broken up and distributed on a fair-share basis around the suburbs on a basis that will "upgrade" Negroes without "downgrading" whites. The con-descension of this is obviously insufferable. At least we have learned that integrating low class Negroes with low class whites is good for neither. The likelihood that we will achieve any massive redistribution of Negroes throughout white sub-urbs is slim. Token do-gooding such as bussing Negro chil-dren to suburban schools in the Boston metropolitan area is likely and it may do some good. With all its difficulties we are probably embarked on a course leading to some, possibly many, black-governed cities. The alternative is some variant of the South African solution, not altogether unlikely although hopefully within our power to avoid.

As in all cases of decolonialization the problem is one of the colonials' capacity to form, sustain, and man a govern-ment. We face the age old problem that when the time has come for self-government, the conditions are not ripe. Negro leadership is lacking. Constituencies to support a stable effec-tive leadership are nonexistent. Trained professionals to man the bureaucracies are lacking. But American cities are far readier than Africa or others newly launched on a career of self-government. It is even now possible that the transition might be eased. Johnson's call for ex-servicemen to prepare themselves and be prepared for service as firemen and police-men is clearly directed at Negroes. If there is any redeeming feature of the Vietnam war, and with all its bloody futility there should be, it is the development of trained, skilled Negroes. These may add to our woefully thin cadres of trained, experienced Negroes. Hopefully, we will not try to use them as mercenaries. The prospect would be more re-assuring if Negro militants did not escalate to Havana and Hanoi. Carmichael's return to the role of a moderate may be untrue, a sell-out, or sanity. Those with the surest sense of the Negroes' need for identity are all too likely to combine that sound insight with apocalyptic fantasies. However, what Joyce Ladner[14] calls the locals, as opposed to these cosmo-politans, have an earthy reality that makes them hopeful.

When all is said, what one hopes for is a revolution in Negroes without a larger revolution. Comparing the Japanese and the Chinese with the Negroes it is easy to see that skin color and discrimination are not the core of the Negroes' problem. The difference between the oriental and the Negro is that however much we may have despised the oriental we never taught him to despise himself. By remaining alien he remained free. He never lost his culture. We got into the skull of the Negro. To overcome his colonial subservience and sense of incompetence whites have to teach him to revolt and finally to adjust to his self-government. Hopefully self-government within the limits of the possible will grow identity, pride, and social structure. With this some decent basis for mutual trade, intercourse, and respect can be created. The white man cannot liberate the Negro. He has to do that himself. What the white man can do is create the conditions where this is less difficult and the conditions where a vindictive South African backlash is less likely.

NOTES

1. Herbert Hill, *Journal of Urban Law* 44 (Winter 1966), 234.
2. Kenneth B. Clark, *Dark Ghetto: Dilemmas of Social Power* (New York: Harper & Row, 1967).
3. James Q. Wilson, *Negro Politics: The Search for Leadership* (New York: The Free Press, 1960).
4. Nathan Glazer and Daniel P. Moynihan, *Beyond the Melting Pot* (Cambridge: M.I.T. Press, 1963), p. 53. See their concern with the Negro middle class, p. 52.
5. Dorothy K. Newman, "The Negro's Journey to the City—Part II," *Monthly Labor Review*, June 1965, p. 648.
6. Peter M. Blau and Otis Dudley Duncan, *The American Occupational Structure* (New York: Wiley, 1967), p. 405.
7. Herman P. Miller, *Rich Man, Poor Man* (New York: Crowell, 1965), Chapter 6.
8. Miller, *Rich Man, Poor Man*, p. 103.
9. Charles E. Silberman, "The City and the Negro," *Fortune*, March 1962.
10. Hill, *Journal of Urban Law*.
11. Bernard Frieden, "Housing and National Urban Goals: Old Policies and New Realities," in *The Metropolitan Enigma*, James Q. Wilson, ed. (Washington, D.C.: Chamber of Commerce of the United States, 1967).
12. Jeffrey K. Hadden, Louis H. Masotti, Victor Thiessen, "The Making of the Negro Mayors, 1967," *Trans-Action*, January–February 1968.
13. Glazer and Moynihan, *Beyond the Melting Pot*, p. 36.
14. Joyce Ladner, "What 'Black Power' Means to Negroes in Mississippi," *Trans-Action*, November 1967.

3 | MARTIN REIN

Social Stability and Black Ghettos

Black power, black capital, and welfare colonialism, as the model to describe the subjugation of black ghettos by whites, are what Don Schon called ideas in good currency, for they are widely accepted by the political right and left. And as do all currencies, they form a common basis for exchange and bargaining in the efforts to develop urban social policy. The commitment to the rhetoric of the redistribution of power and the expansion of citizenship power to command the events which shape their lives are not limited to the eccentric ideal of the student left, the black extremists, and the muddled liberals in search of an ideology. These views are widely shared by many persons widely distributed on the political spectrum. While there is agreement on means, there is much disagreement on the priorities for sorting out our immediate social objectives. This article tries to probe the rationale and aims of the conservative case for black power and black capital.

Conservative political leaders like Nixon have staunchly supported the claims of black power. He has recently suggested that all black militants want is "a share of the wealth and a piece of the action." This required, he said, technical assistance—loan guarantees, new capital sources, incentives to

This chapter is a response to the preceding chapter by Norton E. Long.

44]

industry to provide job training—measures that would help produce the "black ownership" from which would flow "black pride, black jobs, black opportunity, and, yes, black power."[1]

Articles and editorials in the *Wall Street Journal* and *Fortune* magazine have extolled the virtues of Alinsky's efforts to politicalize the poor by the tactics of confrontation and conflict. Organizing "the poor" and organizing "the blacks" may be used interchangeably for they reflect by and large only the different labels that political pragmatists use. In the early years of the delinquency prevention programs (under Kennedy) and the poverty program (under Johnson) it seemed politically unacceptable to have a national program for Black America, while a war against poverty could appeal to all. We thus blurred the distinctions between the issue of race and class. Programs organized on behalf of the latter were often really intended for the former.

Humphrey supported a National Urban Development Bank in which federal funds would help to finance high-risk ghetto businesses, which would help to nourish the incipient efforts at developing black capital. A bipartisan group of Senators (including Harris, Mondale, Ribicoff, and Javits) introduced "The Community Self-Determination Act of 1968," designed to create community-controlled enterprises which would permit the people of the community "to utilize a share of the profits of community-sponsored enterprises to provide needed social services."[2] The auspices of the bill outside of Congress faithfully reflected its hybrid commitment to collectivism and industrialism, for the bill was endorsed and partly created by the efforts of CORE leaders Roy Innis and James Farmer. Finally, the New York Urban Coalition, one of about fifty local coalitions affiliated with the National Urban Coalition, designed to create a local alliance among business, labor, religious, civil rights, and municipal leaders, has created a Task Force on Economic Development. The Task Force has created two corporations, one to provide managerial and technical advice to slum businessmen, and the other to provide short-term financing to ghetto businesses classified by banks as projects of high risk.[3] Recent critiques by Nathan Glazer of the Report of the

Commission on Civil Disorders should also be mentioned
here for they are consistent with the general argument developed so far. Glazer is exercised about what he regards
as one of the glaring omissions in the Commission's report,
namely its failure to take account of the middle-class Negro
and the secure working class Negro in its interpretation of
the causes of urban unrest. "This is the missing man in the
present crisis. And yet he must be a key factor both in the
analysis of the problem . . . and in the solution of the
problem."[4]

Why do conservative political leaders like Nixon support
black power? The Glazer thesis about the missing middle man
hints at the reasons why the political near-right would support what appears to be a program based upon a more radical
ideology. The development of a Negro middle class appeals
to the concerns about social stability, control of lower class
culture, and the restoration of a broken role to enable whites
to negotiate with blacks. Hence there appears to be a powerfully "conservative" network for black power. What Glazer
hints at, Norton E. Long develops into a coherent articulate
analysis.

Norton Long's paper on "Politics and Ghetto Perpetuation"
provides an interpretation of the role of the missing man in
today's urban social unrest and the policy implications which
derive from the analysis. Long's paper is an attempt to
formulate a theory about ghetto instability.

Long's Position

Long's position can be briefly summarized as follows. In
American society other ethnic-commercial enclaves have
created a government and economy of their own and from
this political economic base a social structure has emerged
which assures social stability. However, the pattern in the
Negro community is significantly different. Here a truncated
occupational structure has developed which is dominated by
lower class Negroes, with a noticeable absence of commercial
interests and with control largely residing in the white community. "The Negro middle class until recently has been

escapist (and) . . . where it cannot physically flee it has sought physical coexistence and spiritual isolation. . . . The outstanding fact is that middle class Negroes do not govern the ghetto. They are afraid of it." We thus confront a community with a unique lower class culture made possible by a missing middle class and control by an alien race. The result of the failure of self-government has been a distrust of leaders and the emergence of the lower class as the only authentic and indigenous culture. The combination of these ingredients has produced political instability and an economy of the "hustle," "cashing-in," the welfare dole, and "a social incapacity to mobilize resources." "The costs of a purely lower class culture of immediate consumption have been a failure to make use of the economic avenues of upward mobility."

This, then, is an interpretation of the causes of social unrest. The solution lies in creating a black middle class. A transition of leadership is needed, not dissimilar to the colonial transition when blacks are taught self-government by departing white rulers. "The key question is whether there exists or can rapidly be produced sufficient middle class cadres to govern the black-governed city . . . the greatest fear is clearly that the middle class Negroes . . . cannot dominate the lower class culture of ghetto life." Presumably then, the Negro middle class leadership can more effectively police its own lower class culture if it has both the authority and the capability of exercising that leadership. By altering the truncated structure in black comunities it would be possible "to break the debilitating dependence on white financing."

A somewhat parallel argument can be found in the long tradition in the sociological theory of deviance. In the work of Thomas and Znaniecki near the turn of the twentieth century, and in the research of Shaw and McKay of the Chicago area school of sociologists in the 1930s, in the programs of Social Action financed by the Juvenile Delinquency and Youth Offenses Control Act of 1961, and later by Community Action Programs under the Economic Opportunity Act of 1964, we find a similar theory that the restoration of leadership and authority would contribute toward the creation of greater community cohesion, and thus reduce the problem of immigrant groups, delinquency, and poverty.[5] These various theories and programs for managing the problems of delinquency, crime, and poverty saw the solution in a competent community in which established middle class leadership would be able effectively to control its own affairs, including the policing of its youth. Competence could be achieved through the processes of community organization and citizen participation, for the purposes of leadership development.

The theory then is that an economically integrated and cohesive community is more likely to be a socially stable one. Class, rather than race, seems, according to this interpretation, to be crucial in understanding the sources of social unrest. As individuals improve their situation they leave behind a community lacking in stable leadership and, therefore, unable to control its members, and especially its young. Clearly, there is much to commend this argument.

An Assessment of the Theory and the Policies Based on It

I wish only to pose some questions about the validity, effectiveness, and relevance of the thesis set forth above, which must, in the end, rest on the assumption that the strategies of reform which held in the past apply as well to events today. But at least some of the folowing questions may be posed.

The colonial model calls for a transition period where leadership is transferred from the white to the black community. During the intervening period training for leadership is crucial. However, black leaders criticize the argument because they feel that capability already exists in the ghetto. Perhaps it is unlettered, but it is also shrewdly intelligent with a demonstrated capability of adapting with creativity and ingenuity to an exploitative environment. According to this interpretation social unrest is the product of a revolt against exploitation, rather than the incompetence of the middle class to police and to govern its own lower class.

Yet another objection might be raised concerning the mo-
tive on the part of some white political leaders to encourage
various aspects in the development of black power, namely
the middle man. White America tries to create a black middle
class leadership to act as a broker, as a middle man between
the white and the black community. White political leaders
have no one to negotiate with during periods of confrontation. They are dismayed by a political style which demands
morality and justice but lacks a concrete program with nego-
tiable terms. The insistence on leadership thus arises not so
much from the desire to create an orderly transition from
white domination to black control, but rather out of the wish
to create the machinery in which a dialogue between the
rulers and the ruled can be restored. White society appears
to have lost the capacity to listen, to care, and to respond to
the needs and preferences of black urban America, in accordance with the rules of orderly, incremental change with which
it is familiar.

Thus far I have tried to ask whether the theory is valid
and whether the colonial analogy illuminates or obscures the
underlying motives behind urban social unrest. But even if
we acknowledge the validity of the theory, and respect what
it is, we need to inquire as to whether it can be effective in
the political and economic environment of the 1960s. These
factors will be briefly considered:

1. Class antagonism within the black community is very
deep. Anger against the "Uncle Toms" is quite different
from earlier anger against the "lace curtain Irish," who by
"buying in" were seen as having "sold out." Hence the middle
class broker role may be much harder to play today, both in
terms of policing the lower class and negotiating with the
white middle class. But it is not only that black leaders may
not represent their constituencies; neither can white leaders
deliver programs requiring state and federal resources that
they cannot control locally.

The rise of a Negro middle class if accompanied by the
failure of the lower income groups to improve their relative
situation may create within the black community two nations
as internally divided from each other as are the black from

the white communities. If the rise of the Negro middle class fails to improve the relative position of the lower class as well, the growth of inequalities will result in more instability. The same arguments that apply when whites are compared to blacks hold as well within the Negro community. Reducing inequalities within the Negro community is more crucial in producing tranquility than the creation of an elite middle class. Accordingly, the theory that increased affluence of middle class Negroes contributes toward social stability seems a doubtful proposition. Some attempts to study political instability in developing societies have also demonstrated that a marginal increase in wealth if not accompanied by the reduction of inequalities can lead to political instability.

2. Cities in the United States are suffering a financial, administrative, political, and economic crisis which is as deeply disturbing as the crisis of social unrest and rioting. Thus the transfer of power from whites to blacks may not be much of a prize today. Political control by blacks over a financially starved but decentralized school system or community action program may serve only to intensify the sense of frustration, as those responsible for directing these projects now understand. Moreover, as the conflict between butter and guns intensifies (as witnessed by the 6-billion-dollar expenditure cut by the Federal government) the amount of resources to urban schools and poverty programs may in the face of inflation and rising populations actually decline, thus forcing these benefit systems to act as rationing devices in the distribution of scarcity. Some economists feel that the military budget in the post-Vietnam era will not be substantially reduced. Accordingly, if no effective pressure for reducing military expenditure is developed even after the war, the clash between bread and guns may continue. Rationing of social services will, of course, require further exclusion from institutions and the intensification of the alienation which black control is designed to reduce.

But curiously, social progress as well as urban failure make the transfer to black power even more difficult. "Fifty years of social reform," Moynihan asserted, "has pretty well destroyed the basis of working class politics in this country."[6]

He was, of course, referring to those reforms which were aimed at breaking the power of political bosses to distribute patronage by their control of city jobs. Thus the creation of Civil Service Commissions was designed at least in principle to assure that impartial criteria were used in the hiring of public officials. Clearly efforts are being made to reverse these patterns. We have come to learn the socially useful functions of what earlier liberal reformers defined as corruption. Moynihan persuasively presents the case:

Having destroyed the power of the local bosses, we learn that the people feel powerless. Having put an end to patronage and established merit systems in civil service, we find the poor unqualified and without jobs. Having banished felons from public employment, we find enormous numbers of men who need jobs have criminal records.[7]

There has been an assault on these liberal reforms. For example, credentialism has been challenged as a criterion of exclusion, rather than a measure of quality. Instead, we have been urged to use performance criteria. One rationale to support this position can be briefly summarized. Employers have tended to overdefine the competencies which are needed to perform occupational jobs, hence our trained workers are more likely to experience frustrations which affect the quality of their work. The lowering of academic and social standards may thus enhance rather than erode the quality of employment outputs. The greater efficiency of ghetto controlled services was cogently presented in an article in the *New York Times*, July 17, 1968.

A hospital worker serving a local Negro administrator may demand no more in wages than he obtained from an absentee bureaucracy, but he may deliver more services. A pupil in a school administered by a board of local citizens may cost no more to educate than now, but the pupil may find the experience more relevant. His education, thus, may become more productive.

Ghetto control of social services may not be feasible if nonprofessionals are not recruited to man the social services bureaucracies. The hiring of nonprofessionals and the bypassing of the Civil Service requirements are also illustrative of this trend away from credentialism. If control of social services, jobs, and education is won it seems unlikely that the whole pattern will be reversed. Thus black power may have few resources to distribute the kind of patronage on which the exercise of political leadership must depend.

3. Changes in the economy will make it more difficult to promote the ideals of black capital self-help and self-sufficiency. The creation of black capital will largely be encouraged by stimulating the development of small business by reserving the Negro market for Negro businesses. But the commitment to the resuscitation of small business in the ghetto will pose substantial problems. For one thing, all small business tends to have a high death rate, and there is every reason to assume that the rates of business failures within the Negro community will be as high as they are in the rest of the community, if not higher. Second, according to Andrew Bremmer, as the size of the middle income group (annual family income of $7,000) expands to half of the Negro families, as it now is among whites, "the large national corporations will find the Negro market increasingly attractive. Thus, these corporations are not about to withdraw and allow the Negro businessman to treat the Negro market as his special preserve."[8] It seems doubtful that a clash between the needs of black and white capital will redound to the benefit of blacks.

It is also unlikely that the discussion about locating more plants of large industrial firms in the ghetto, and creating more jobs as well as a black economic elite not rooted in the ownership of capital but in its management, will go very far. There has been a continued exit of manufacturing industries from central cities for the past twenty-five years because it is simply not sufficient for low capital, high labor-intensive industry to function on the high land and tax rates in center cities.[9]

Finally, of course, account must be taken of the changing distribution in the occupational structure, which, while it has not altogether eliminated the need for unskilled labor nor created the disjunction between work and earnings which some have claimed, has nevertheless reduced the need for the kinds of skills for which Negroes are most heavily employed today. This trend will lead toward more public employment rather than the development of black capital or decentralized private corporations. But even if the creation of black capital with its intended emphasis on self-help and self-sufficiency were successful, it is much more likely to create greater economic interdependency between the white and the black community and hence a more subtle form of economic control. In periods of rapid economic expansion (the gross national product increased by more than 40 billion dollars in the first half of 1968), industry may be willing to buy stability at a *token* level by encouraging the development of black capital through loan guarantees, technical assistance and other devices. But as the size of the Negro population grows (Bremmer's argument) or as fluctuations in the economy produce periods of recession and a decline in industrial profits, then economic realities may force a reassessment of the acceptability of the principle of "black capital." In these periods of economic decline, white economic domination of the ghetto may become visible, and anger will be directed, not only against welfare colonialism and political control of the ghetto, but against white capitalism as well.

If this interpretation is valid it would seem important to reach out to the economic citadels in the white community and to tackle directly the problem of prejudice, especially in the professional, managerial, and white collar jobs. The legal machinery needed to open up rather than wall off society is already in hand. A good deal of legislation has already been won which assures the Negro the right to vote, the right to equal treatment in the courts, the right of access to all publicly financed services, and the right to equal employment and open housing. But we have failed to provide the regulatory agencies with the power, the staffing, and the financial support which would permit them to implement these objectives.

Finally, we turn to the relevance of Long's argument. We need to consider whether the missing man thesis distorts the priorities of public policy by directing its attention to the problems of stability rather than justice. While it is true that the liberal, the militant, and the conservative have all directed their attention to black power, the goals they seek are after all quite different. One group is interested in a transfer of power. They want different actors to fill the present slots in the structure which distributes the positions of power and authority and influence. The new actors ought to be middle class blacks rather than middle class whites. In the transfer power strategy one major goal seems to be that of social stability and one major obstacle seems to be lack of competence, following Long's analysis. There is fear on the part of the whites that power will be transferred without capability. What is wanted by the whites is competent blacks who can act as power brokers negotiating with the white community in terms that will "cool out" the ghetto.

But for other groups, more than a transfer of power to achieve social stability is being sought. Black power and student power have much in common in their search for a different society. They argue that the roots of this American society which has produced the Vietnam war and the Negro crisis must themselves be poisoned. They are critical of the nature and uses of power. (Senator Fulbright has also in a different context called attention to the social costs of the arrogance of power.) Students almost the world over are concerned with the arbitrary use of authority, the process of dehumanization associated with bureaucratization, what Buber called the drift to I-It relationships instead of I-Thou relationships, where people are used as instrumentalities to augment personal objectives. They want to tear the roots out and to plant afresh. But they are uncertain about what new seeds are needed to create blossoms of love, justice, and humanity. The older radicals assumed that the need for authority and bureaucracy would wither away in the good society. But if these are the very source of evil and the withering theory is repudiated, then we are left with either cynicism or ideals that lack a program. The former leads to dropping out and the latter to a revolution without a platform.

The "search for the missing man" (Negro middle class leadership) approach to the urban crises is misleading because it is incomplete. This is not to argue against black power, but only to say that as a strategy it is incomplete and hence misleading. Power without purpose is insufficient. Because of these doubts I am led to the position that action at this point should be more preoccupied with probing tactics than with fundamental principles. We have already witnessed fads in public policy concerning Negroes; social movements may also succumb to fadism. Black power *may* languish into tomorrow's world, while the problems remain unheeded.

Perhaps then the only viable policy to pursue is an inconsistent one, simultaneously directed at the break-up of and the strengthening of the ghetto. To break up the ghetto, social policy must emphasize the reduction of inequalities of income; full employment, not on the average, but for special groups (such as ghetto residents and Negro youth), and a vigorous program to reduce what Bayard Rustin called "institutional racism rather than personal racism" by creating "social and economic institutions in which all peoples have a sense of identification."[10]

Even if the theory of the missing man is valid, it does not follow that the solutions in a changing political, economic, and class situation can be derived from social policies designed to restore the missing man into an economically integrated community. There is asymmetry in the development of policy, since the solution of the problems may be better achieved by methods other than those which attack the causes frontally. But in the absence of evidence which can support or refute the theory it is perhaps best to pursue it along with other policies which are based on different assumptions. I would support, in short, a politics of inconsistency.

NOTES

1. *The New York Times,* May 19, 1968.
2. *Congressional Record,* Senate, July 24, 1966, p. S.270.
3. *The New York Times,* June 11, 1968.
4. Nathan Glazer, "The Problem with American Cities," *New Society,* March 21, 1968.
5. For a discussion of this theory see Peter Marris and Martin Rein, *Dilemmas of Social Reform: Poverty and Community Action in the United States* (New York: Atherton Press, 1967).

6. Daniel P. Moynihan, "The Politics of Stability," a paper presented at the National Board Meeting, Americans for Democratic Action, September 23, 1967.
7. *The New York Times,* June 5, 1968.
8. Quoted from a commencement address presented by Mr. Andrew F. Bremmer, a Negro member of the Federal Reserve Board, at Clark College. *The New York Times,* June 4, 1968.
9. For discussion of some of these issues, see Sumner M. Rosen's account of "Better Mousetrap: Reflections on Economic Development in the Ghetto," mimeographed.
10. *The New York Times,* April 28, 1968.

COMMENTS: NORTON E. LONG

I BELIEVE Professor Rein misreads an important part of my argument. This may be my fault for not being sufficiently clear. I hope the following few lines will set things straight.

Professor Rein sees me as a protagonist of the "missing man" argument. In this view, the failure of the Negro middle class to play their role in the ghetto accounts for its social disorganization. The return of the middle class or in any event the development of a substantial middle class playing its role in the ghetto is seen as the major remedy for the present condition.

The thesis I intended to propose, however, accounts for middle class absenteeism in terms of Negro lower class culture as described by Kenneth Clark. It sees the problem of social disorganization in the ghetto as arising not so much from the "missing man" as from the missing roles in Negro lower class culture. My argument is essentially that Negro lower class culture, unlike the lower class cultures of other ethnic groups, is devoid of legitimate control roles. The absence of legitimate control roles deprives lower class Negroes of a necessary means of social organization.

Whereas other ethnic lower class migrants, even when without any of their ethnic middle class with them, could promote fellow lower class ethnics to control roles in their culture normally held by middle class people, the Negro lower class has a subculture in which there are no legitimate control roles to promote lower class members to. Indeed, the absence of legitimate control roles in Negro lower class culture debars middle class Negroes from filling such roles. When they attempt to, they are regarded as white agents or, in any event, as illegitimate.

I find in the lack of legitimate control roles in the Negro lower class subculture the most satisfactory explanation of the peculiar characteristics of the Negro ghetto and its perpetuation. Likewise, I see the development of legitimate control roles in Negro lower class culture as a necessary condition for overcoming the social disorganization of the ghetto, a prime cause of its peculiar powerlessness. I see in variants of nationalism and the models of decolonialization suggestive analogies. These analogies point to how populations without a legitimate structure of control roles may acquire one and develop, either from elements of their middle or lower class or both, personnel to fill the newly created roles.

4 | ROBERT C. WOOD

The Ghettos and
Metropolitan Politics

The dynamics of metropolitan growth and change do not lend themselves to simple explanations or prescriptions. If there were only a few dragons in our path, we would already have laid them low. If money alone could guarantee the American urban future, perhaps even the 90th Congress would have found its way to the rainbow's end.

The following discussion is based on three premises:

First, that our efforts over the last forty years to diagnose and cope with "the metropolitan problem" have gone through at least three phases—each of them useful but limited and faulty.

Second, that the past five years have seen major progress both in our national commitment to urban problems and in our capacity to build a genuine metropolitan community.

Third, that it is in community, based on social justice, and not in separatism, voluntary or otherwise, that the future of our metropolitan areas—and hence our nation—must be found.

The Cities and the Suburbs

There is nothing new about the suburban impulse. The exodus of the more affluent from the noise, congestion, and indifference of the city began almost as soon as the cities themselves. Nineteenth-century New York merchants and professionals built town houses in the then-pastoral precincts of Greenwich Village. Well before the Spanish-American War Philadelphia's upper class moved farther and farther out along the Main Line railroad.

Until World War I, this outflow was a relative trickle and the municipal government remained the arena for confrontation between immigrant and old-timer. The suburban land boom of the 1920s, however, swept significant numbers of old-timers out of reach of municipal problems and taxes. High-priced suburbs like Beverly Hills, Shaker Heights, Grosse Pointe Park, and Bronxville multiplied in population several times over. Around the nation's seventeen largest cities, the suburban population increased by 40 percent over the decade, and developers and their private transit company allies gobbled up every field in sight. Enough land was subdivided on Long Island to house the entire metropolitan population of New York; enough around Chicago to handle that city's growth for twenty years.[1]

The Depression rewarded much of this optimism with bankruptcy, but the suburban pattern was sufficiently established for astute observers to detect governmental chaos on the horizon. Early metropolitan reformers frequently saw the key metropolitan problem as one of central-city corruption. If the suburban communities could only band together to reform and enlighten the city folk dedicated to "government of the people, by the rascals, for the rich" then orderly growth and metropolitan bliss and togetherness might be assured.[2]

What these evangelists overlooked—in addition to the indifference of both suburb and city to the proposed scenario—was emerging political leadership within the cities themselves. Men like La Guardia were already beginning to prove that answers to the problems of big city government were to be found not in the antisepsis of procedural reform—imposed from in or outside—but in the *realpolitik* of conflicting interest groups.

If the diagnoses were mistaken, the premonitions of metropolitan chaos were not. Underwritten by World War II's pent-up demand, the urban middle class exploded across the city limits in the late 1940s.

The single-family house-and-lot (described by Max Ways as "a mini-farmhouse behind a mini-meadow where no mule grazes"), the ranch-style school, the industrial plant designed like a country club became the hallmarks of land-rich America. Inspired by a small town ethos, the new suburban communities reinforced their homogeneity with zoning and building codes and underscored their independence with a jealous insistence on political separation. The sharp Balkanization of the suburbs was further complicated by the creation of thousands of "special districts" whose boundaries casually overlapped municipal and county lines. Between 1942 and 1967, over 13,000 new single-function districts were created to handle services ranging from water supply and sanitation to cemeteries.

A few—but precious few—cities were able to pursue a vigorous policy of annexation, keeping the city limits more remote than the demands for new fringe housing. More often, however, annexation efforts were too little and too late, with central-city councils the losers in confrontations with hard-nosed suburban mayors.

The resulting mosaics of overlapping, competitive jurisdictions were clearly an affront to economy and efficiency, and the 1950s' diagnosis of "the metropolitan problem" centered on just such businessmen's values. The strong thrust for "metro government" was basically a call for a more business-like production of urban goods and services. It was aimed at quantity discounts and the prevention of waste.

After a high tide of success in the metropolitan experiments of Toronto and Miami, reorganization proposals were voted down in city after city. With the 1959 defeats in St. Louis and Cleveland, the drive for formal metropolitan government more or less struck out. While the 1963 Nashville–Davidson County restructuring has suggested new possibilities, simple patterns of local governmental reforms are obviously not the most popular item on America's political agenda.

In retrospect it seems clear that the "metro" believers underestimated the depth of the suburbanite's indifference and hostility to the city and the tenacity of his identification with the new turf. The out-migrant middle class really did not want a reunion. Its new ranch houses, barbecue pits, and motorboats represented the successful climax in a long search for identity within a smaller, more tranquil and more like-minded community.

Identity-seeking alone, of course, cannot explain the Great Suburban Migration. Alienation from city politics, rising taxes, war-sparked affluence, federally supported home mortgages, the lure of speculative profits, the symbiotic growth of highways and car ownership, and—clearly not least—fear of the city's growing nonwhite population, formed a powerful collective push-pull which changed the face of the nation.

By 1960, the change was established and largely irreversible. The 1940 Census identified 140 metropolitan areas, covering about 45,000 square miles and including about 48 percent of the country's population. In 1960, there were 212 areas, covering 310,00 square miles and including 63 percent of the population.

Most central cities barely maintained their populations, or suffered an absolute decline, during these years. The growth was suburban growth. Between 1950 and 1960, while the New York metropolitan area gained over two million residents, Manhattan and Brooklyn lost 370,000.

Crisis in Black and White

It is the nature of these widespread population shifts that has produced this decade's diagnosis of the "metropolitan problem." For hidden within the slowly declining statistics of the central city were more dramatic changes: the departure of substantial numbers of white families and the arrival of a similar number of nonwhite families.

The families who left were those who could afford suburban real estate. Those who replaced them were largely poor and inexperienced in urban living. The changes placed increasing stress on the creaking political and economic structure of our aging cities. Quite suddenly, in the mid-60s, these changes and stresses began to arouse general public concern.

Marquis Childs has compared the report of the National Advisory Commission on Civil Disorders to the handwriting on the wall that confronted the roisterers at the feast of Belshazzar.[3] Without diminishing the importance of the Commission's warnings in any way I would point out that the handwriting regarding urban apartheid has been visible for some time. Morton Grodzins and Edward Banfield described the pattern more than a decade ago.[4] Several of us measured and documented it.[5] If ever social science lived up to its predictive power, even with relatively crude statistical instruments, it was in the late 1950s when it forecast the development of the white suburban "noose" and the Negro urban "heartland."

Predictable or no, these developments have caused many in the past few years to view "the metropolitan problem" almost solely in terms of race. But this diagnosis is also faulty, or at least dangerously incomplete. To devote our total attention to the debate of Black vs. White, of dispersal vs. gilded ghettos, is to mistake the basic cause of metropolitan problems and the basic purpose of metropolitan reform. It is also to court an unproductive paranoia.

Urban professionals have a particular responsibility to talk sense to the American people and to each other regarding the sources of our metropolitan dilemmas. To christen every deteriorating neighborhood a ghetto, to blame official racism for the economics of the housing market, to see malice in suburban indifference and racial exploitation in every small business mark-up will serve neither the truth nor the community.

The patterns of metropolitan institutions provoke injustice and discrimination, but the pressures behind those patterns are far more complex than race alone.

The way in which factories, jobs, and people are distributed across the metropolitan landscape is not a mystery and it is not a conspiracy. Urban growth hinges on classic economic factors of entrepreneurship, capital, labor, and natural resources. Decisions on plant location can be traced to considerations of comparative advantage in transportation facilities, local business taxes, utility rates, land costs, and labor supply. Residential land values are based on location, topography, zoning, and available services and amenities. The science of urban economics is still young, but we are learning steadily about how urban areas grow and how they can stay healthy.

Ten years ago, in his pioneering studies of New York,[6] Raymond Vernon described how "every area of the metropolitan region is forever being tested and retested for its most efficient economic use." As the highway network and truck transportation freed manufacturers from dependence on the dock or railsiding, and food processors from the need to be close to their customers, these "space-eaters" moved out to the metropolitan fringe. The high rents and high wages of the urban core increasingly dictate industries with high return even though core residential neighborhoods become slums. They include highly complex industries like finance, television, dress design that require a "face-to-face" convergence of specialists from many different fields or the special intersection of transportation facilities which the city provides. Between the downtown and the fringe, commercial and industrial areas tend to be occupied by marginal enterprises, or old establishments which for one reason or another have not faced the cost and trouble of relocation. Certain industries create residential patterns by their location; others follow where their consumers lead.[7]

Race and discrimination have certainly influenced the patterns of population distribution in metropolitan areas. But they have not created these patterns so much as they have sharpened them and made them more conspicuous. Central cities contain the oldest housing, and older housing has traditionally sheltered those with the least to spend: the elderly, the retired, and those who are disadvantaged in the local labor market—the handicapped, the uneducated, the unskilled, and the urban newcomer. With the in-migration of low-income families and the expansion of the downtown commercial district, frankly deteriorating, low-income city neighborhoods spread to confront the surrounding aging "gray areas"—often 50- to 75-year-old suburbs. Racial differences have heightened the conflicts along these changing boundaries which historically have seldom been peaceful. Modern suburban zoning —large lots and high construction standards—have been aimed at keeping away the white poor as well as the black, but discrimination against the black middle class has increased the visibility of class lines. New minimum standard houses on minimum lots beyond the periphery of urban zoning *will* become available to Negro families, with a powerful assist by the Civil Rights Act of 1968. But its fringe location makes it primarily attractive to someone whose job tenure is secure and whose work location is unlikely to change.

None of this is intended to excuse the continued blight of discrimination. To realize how recently separate school systems, segregated municipal facilities, restrictive covenants, and "white primaries" were accepted urban practice is to marvel at our collective indecency.

Lyndon Johnson's Secretary of Housing and Urban Development grew up and was educated in his native Washington, D.C., in a Negro school system—buildings, administration, teaching staff—completely separate. In the 1930s, he integrated, for the first time in American history, a federal government cafeteria. In the 1940s he could not eat at any downtown restaurant except the Union Station and the YWCA. Down to the 1950s movie houses, theaters, bowling alleys, playgrounds, and swimming pools remained strictly segregated.

But Robert Weaver was Lyndon Johnson's Secretary of the Department of Housing and Urban Development, charged, among other responsibilities, with the first administration of the Fair Housing provisions of the Civil Rights Act of 1968.

The Negro experience in urban America has been one of prolonged outrage, and the sharp impatience of the urban black community must be read against that fact. The point is not that we should condone past injustice but that we should confront it with the fullest possible understanding of the metropolitan dynamic.

The metropolitan area is the political arena of the future. It will be the home of virtually all of the 100 million additional Americans expected by the end of the century. The social welfare agenda reached at this forum and the program of HUD and other Federal agencies must be made operative in a metropolitan context.

Some Signs of Movement

While I am not sanguine, I am unfashionably optimistic about our metropolitan future and about our capacity to surmount poverty and injustice. This optimism is grounded in the growing national commitment to urban problems and in the increasing local capacity to respond to that commitment.

Just two years ago, HUD was a new creation. Model Cities was given little chance of passage. Rent supplements had squeaked through Congress but had absolutely no funds. Our working relations—urbanists and social welfare professionals— were tentative and insecure. A classic meeting with the late Howard Gustafson, whose brilliant career was tragically cut short that week, Fern Colborn, Charles Schottland, and Melvin Glasser began a process of powerful, helpful collaboration.

In the interim—as you may have noticed—we have not solved the urban problems. Our areas of ignorance, inadequacy, and insensitivity remain large and stubborn, including those of the federal establishment. These two years, however, have seen substantial progress in legislation, financial commitment, and awareness at the national level.

Three major housing bills have equipped us not only with Model Cities but with metropolitan planning incentives, assistance to new communities, support for urban research and training, greatly increased flexibility in the provision of low-rent housing, and interest rate subsidies to permit home ownership by low-income families. The Civil Rights bill of 1968 has added considerably to our ability to ensure open occupancy in both sales and rentals.

HUD's annual expenditures—apart from mortgage support— have tripled and stand in the new budget at $2,750,000,000.

Probably most important (and of course the riots and black militancy played a role in this), both Congress and the public have come to take seriously the problems of the cities, and they are not unsophisticated about the nature of those problems.

So we are finally making major urban commitments. We have charted a ten-year housing program which can produce 6 million subsidized units and eliminate all substandard housing within the next decade. Model Cities is in part a demonstration program. As we discover what works, what kind of arrangements we have to make in order to bring our resources to bear on the inner city, these resources—public and private —will have to be invested on a large scale. This investment will probably be forthcoming.

The one essential resource, however, will still remain the capacity of the city—the metropolitan area—to make use of available money, knowledge, and experience; to guide and survive social change; to get things done in a sustained, deliberate, sensitive way. There are grounds for optimism here in the emergence of genuine metropolitan political systems.

In many metropolitan areas we are witnessing collaborative activities by local governments and interest groups which extend beyond metropolitan libraries or shared police communications into the more difficult questions of land use and resource allocation. The rudiments of a political system—a communications network, an array of activists expressing their interest and engaging in negotiations, and a set of goals distinct from the particular interests of any participant—are present, albeit tentative and informal.

But the outcome remains uncertain. We are still learning how to put together metropolitan coalitions; we are still seeking ways to make metropolitan decision-making responsive to the public will; we do not yet know how to ameliorate what Marshall Kaplan calls "the historical weaknesses of the poor in playing the resource allocation game."

The questions to be posed regarding the ghetto and metropolitan politics are:

First, is this admittedly embryonic, evolving metropolitan political system—with many participants, without formal structure, too often dependent on federal money and federal programs for decisive action—strong enough to deal with deep divisions of race and class?

And second, can the system move fast enough to make a difference in the terrible interlocked problems of the ghetto, or will it be overwhelmed by them?

We are witnessing, in our metropolitan areas, a conflict between two deep-rooted American traditions. One, born of slavery, is the spurious cult of Negro inferiority. The other is the genuine commitment to an open society.

Southern Bourbonism, the society rooted in the first tradition, was defeated militarily in the bloodiest war in our history. But the cult survives and has arrived with the Negro in the North. Our established national aspiration is the non-aristocratic society, based on open access and assimilation. But the melting pot metaphor has always belied the truth of savage jealousies and painful accommodations.

The cult of inferiority finds its metropolitan representation in the white "garrison suburbs," in the intransigence of old ethnic neighborhoods, in hysterical responses to school bussing or scattered-site public housing—but not in these alone. Black national separatism represents this tradition—inverted. And those, white and Negro, who celebrate the future of black-governed, all-black cities, might ponder whether this is not a new and subtle version of "the back of the bus."

Our cities have always been the stages for our highest culture and the sites of our greatest monuments. But at least for twenty years they have also been the receptacles for the people and the functions that nobody else wanted. They encompass the most obsolete real estate, the worst tax base, and the greatest needs for public expenditure. If we piously give over the job of rebuilding the inner city to the black community, and then abandon these people, we have not only given them the worst, the hardest job. We have almost certainly condemned them to failure.

In the last analysis, we must go the way of metropolitan community—not only because of the blunt facts of economic interdependence but because separatism cannot produce social justice. The metropolitan tendency toward income fragmentation as well as political fragmentation provokes a situation of gross inequalities—in education, taxes, the whole social infra-structure—not only between city and suburbs but between low- and high-income suburbs. For a wide range of local gov-ernment functions—health services, public assistance, subsi-dized housing, school lunches, summer camps—the city and the low-income suburb both need more and have less. If the middle class suburbs renounce their metropolitan responsibili-ties, these programs, which in effect transfer income from one group to another by public action, must eventually be assigned to the county, state, or federal government. The result will be to diminish the power and purpose and impact of local government—black or white.

Martin Luther King, Jr., has written that "there is no sep-arate black path to power and fulfillment that does not intersect white paths, and there is no separate white path to power and fulfillment, short of social disaster, that does not share that power with black aspirations for freedom and human dignity. We are bound together in a single garment of destiny."[8]

The quality of our metropolitan future turns on the recog-nition of this common destiny.

NOTES

1. The course of suburban development is treated in Chapter 2 of Robert C. Wood, *Suburbia* (Boston: Houghton Mifflin, 1958).
2. The phrase "government . . . rich" is from Lincoln Steffens, *Auto-biography* (New York: Harcourt, Brace, 1931), p. 494. Paul Studen-ski (*The Government of Metropolitan Areas,* New York: National Municipal League—Committee on Metropolitan Government, 1930) was among the earliest advocates of metropolitan reform.
3. *The Washington Post,* March 4, 1968.
4. Edward C. Banfield and Morton Grodzins, "Housing Policy and the Government of Metropolitan Areas," report prepared for ACTION, December, 1956.
5. See particularly the volumes on *Race and Residence*, edited by David McIntire, and the New York Metropolitan Region Study.
6. Edgar M. Hoover and Raymond Vernon, *Anatomy of a Metropolis* (Cambridge: Harvard University Press, 1959), is the most relevant here of the nine volumes which comprise the New York Metropoli-tan Region Study.
7. Wilbur R. Thompson, *A Preface to Urban Economics* (Baltimore:

70]   ROBERT C. WOOD

Johns Hopkins Press, 1965), presents a provocative cyclical thesis on the growth process of industries and of urban centers. The discussion which follows draws in part on his analysis.

8. Martin Luther King, Jr., *Where Do We Go From Here: Chaos or Community?* (New York: Harper & Row, 1967).

5 | JAMES R. DUMPSON

Fantasy and Reality
in the Ghetto Problem

It would be nice to be able to agree with those who are optimistic about the metropolitan future, about the national commitment to urban problems, and about the increasing local capacity to respond to that commitment. Robert Wood takes the position that economic interdependence demands we go the way of the metropolitan community, and affirms that social justice cannot be achieved by separatism of any kind. My over-all interpretation is somewhat different.

Industrialization introduced many new variables to the urban scene. The cities were given over to industries that located near existing routes of trade. The toll of this mechanization has been tremendous. Countless vehicles and smoke-stacks spew filth and the agents of deterioration of both persons and property. And the emotional deterioration of hordes of people living a fast life of impersonal interaction can never be measured.

At the same time industrialization was contaminating the cities, it gave impetus to an enlarging of the middle class, which in increasing numbers could afford to leave the city. Improved roads and rapid transportation facilitated their exodus; and as fast as farmland contiguous to the city could be converted into bungalows, the people were there to buy them.

This chapter is a response to the preceding chapter by Robert C. Wood.

Purgatory—Temporary and Permanent

For many people city life came to represent a purgatorial existence which was commuted by affluence. Similarly, it was a springboard through which the poor and minority groups could advance along the continuum of middleclass-ness toward rising status, one goal of which was withdrawal from the city that made their affluence possible. The urban-suburban process became a crisis when our visible minority groups—the Negroes and Puerto Ricans—inherited or predom-inated in the hulks of the cities that had served as the incuba-tors for other emerging groups, and discovered that they were anchored there. The credentials they needed for exit were excessive and unalterable: the political and economic develop-ment upon which group success depends was cut off from them, as were too, the probabilities of success even if the necessities were achieved. The city became for these people, blacks and other minorities, a purgatory made permanent.

So with the introduction of static minority groups came an abrupt stoppage of the migratory pattern. The urban whites who are middle class and above stay for convenience and other personal reasons; those whites who are poor can be comforted by expectation of improvement, if not for them-selves, for their children.

The American economic creed assumes that the sum total of individual selfishness and ruthlessness somehow produces the public good. Most of us come out of the tradition which accepted this notion and have been willing to test ourselves against the impediments of the economic system for a share of success: this is the economic order. However, when to this jungle philosophy has been added prejudicial discrimination against irrelevant factors of race or ethnic background, then it becomes, simply stated, racist.

Drawing on one of Robert Wood's quotes from Marshall Kaplan, America has institutionalized the "resource allocation game." Besides individuals vying against one another, states are in the game against other states; and all the myriad local subdivisions within the states are contesting for their shares. Even agencies within larger governmental units—federal, state, and local—compete for money, and tacitly, for the integrity of their programs and for their very existence.

Against this backdrop, talk of social justice has a hollow echo. Given the atmosphere of social competition in our culture, almost everyone at one time or another suffers exploitation of some form. This is inherent in the system; it is tolerated, and encouraged perhaps by law and certainly by custom. And when practices operate within the sanction of law and custom, how can they be unjust?

But they are definitely immoral when measured against our cultural idealism. This is a fair way of characterizing the plight of the ghettos: they are peopled by those who have no clear options for leaving, and in staying are subjected to a life of socially imposed immorality.

And we have now an urban crisis which is not absolute, but relative and conditional, or, if you will, psychological. The poor Negro or Puerto Rican or Mexican-American is probably better fed, better clothed, better housed, and in better physical condition than his Irish or Eastern European counterpart of a century ago. Compared to the Indian or some Europeans, he lives a life of comparative comfort: however, related to the progress of the rest of America and to the resources, expectations, and promises that have been extended to him, his situation is intolerable.

As Robert Wood has pointed out, money alone is not the answer. Money runs the gambit of allocation according to political realities, which have demonstrably failed to meet our urban challenge. Money fed into the existing structure, regardless of how well intended, is just more finger-in-the-dikesmanship. It does not answer to the mental underpinning of our culture that supports provincialism, which has as just one feature, the continuation of the ghetto. It does not take into perspective the larger issue of what Dr. Kenneth Clark calls "the monkey on America's back"—sentimental attachment to Jeffersonian democracy. Read into this concept is fragmented government; suspicion of city life as indecent and corrupting; praise of the rural life as virtuous and fulfilling; and most mischievous of all, constant vigilance of local interests against federal encroachment, which today can be translated as against national interests. This is a perfect form for governing by tobacco farmers and small-town professional men, and our present Congress retains the flavor. However, it is now a luxury which we can ill afford.

In the description of Model Cities by Robert Wood, what mention was given to planning; not regional or local planning but massive, national plans? There was none, as in truth there could be none. No administrator would dare speculate on the course of this country's cities or other human problems for the next ten years—or even how his agency's program will effectively mesh with others today. Equally, no president has attempted to rock the pork barrel by suggesting seriously that this planning should begin by integrating the efforts of all governmental agencies at every level. Talk of this sort, even though it may have promising results, rings of socialism, and that is, of course, anathema.

Alternatives to Current Policy

But were we to elevate our thinking out of the mire of tradition, alternatives now considered radical might be feasible. Why must we continue the resource-allocation grab-bag game when the fabric of what we are trying to preserve is obsolete and irrational, although in the "best" tradition? It may be that the concept of cities is really outdated. If their function as commercial hubs validates their existence, the potential of our transportation system long ago robbed this claim of substance. Perhaps we should cease trying to refine and update the Elizabethan poor laws into an effective means of providing for the ghettos' casualties.

Consider the futility of both planned and existing federal programs in the context of this appraisal by Jake Ayres, a Negro community leader at Glen Allen, Mississippi.

Putting money into the ghettos while not spending anything, or enough, here will just make bigger ghettos. If they put money up there, and conditions get a little better while nothing is changing here, just one thing will happen. More of our people will leave for the city to take advantage of whatever is done. If they want to do something about the ghettos, they ought to do something big here first.[1]

How do we deal with this procession? Shall we try to pump enough money into Model Cities to at once arrest existing deterioration and forestall its spread? Do we bolster up our welfare services with additional money and personnel for the onslaught, only to precipitate another round? Open up more job training centers to train more people for marginal or obsolete jobs; and Head Start centers to teach ghetto youth to read about Dick and Spot? Do we, in other words, go on with more of the same?

Imagine that tomorrow the Congress passed a bill which guaranteed a minimum income to every American. Suppose that this income were large enough to assure an adequate level of health, nutrition, and housing; and suppose that this, being a federal law, projected a uniform national income with no built-in compensation for regional index of living variations. How might this new law affect that flow of people that was just mentioned?

We can speculate that this measure alone might remove the need for the migration. Further, it would create a disinclination for people to remain in the ghetto, or more generally, for marginal income people to remain in the city at all. If the federal government's plan were, then, uniform, it would be a positive incentive for people to move to areas where this income would give them the highest possible standard of living. Therefore, the marginal or impoverished urban dweller would gain in one stroke the two things he lacks now: money and mobility. Is this an argument for income maintenance? Yes, but in a larger sense, it is an argument for considering— seriously considering—tentative solutions, which do not necessarily originate within the traditional bureaucratic process, to problems that may be caused or prolonged by this process.

As a first effort toward seriousness, we should begin to define terms. Carlyle, in writing his history of the French revolution, pointed out that all revolutions have their origin in the dictionary, and we can continue his precedent in our social revolution. We could start with basics, to wit, poverty. The poor are poor only because they have no money; not because they are shiftless, improvident, decadent, and atheists. And not, by god, because they want to be. If we can just assume this simple reality, the solution is more than indicated: provide them with money or the avenue of a meaningful job to earn it; not burden them with the administrative vanities created for them by the poverty industry's technocrats.

We can reiterate the now hackneyed comparison between our national effort in our two wars, and ask if the war on poverty is really war or just another police action. The Model Cities program, which is an analogue to the pacification program in our "other war," has what sounds like an impressive budget of 1¾ billion dollars, which is a trifle next to its counterpart in the "other war." By comparison, Wilbur Mills can get the Arkansas River project funded for at least one billion dollars; and we spend more than twice this amount on agricultural price support programs. It is particularly sobering to realize that the entire Model Cities budget represents the amount of money necessary to purchase about two square blocks of Park Avenue.

The new housing program calls for erection of 6 million subsidized housing units in the next decade, and at that rate 18 million by the year 2000. How adequate will this be for existing needs plus the needs of 100 million additional Americans in that time?

Next, we in the socially oriented professions might well lose our complacency about the efficacy of social science. Robert Wood vaunts the idea that "social science lived up to its predictive power, even with crude statistical instruments . . . in the late 1950s when it forecast the development of the white suburban 'noose' and the Negro urban 'heartland.' " For earlier predictive material, we could have used DuBois' history of *The Philadelphia Negro*, dating back 50 years before; or Frederick Law Olmstead's *Slave States*, written 100 years before. Or we could have read any social observer like Dickens or Mayhew to arrive at the same prediction without benefit of any statistical tools. It is, it seems to me, a universal tendency for urban poor, regardless of color, to be herded into inner-city slum living from which they rarely emerge. This applies as much to Calcutta and Buenos Aires as it does to New York.

In the same vein, Robert Wood states that the Congress and the public "are not unsophisticated about the nature of those problems" of the cities. What is the assurance of this new-found sophistication? What has changed? Has everyone read or attended to the President's Commission report? If so, nothing is new. The same material has been published about every riot since 1919 and on it goes. Of course, he may have meant sophistical, in which case he is being absolutely candid and perceptive.

Writing *The Folklore of Capitalism,* in 1936, Thurmond Arnold captured the spirit of the study-and-commission routine that even then was a time-honored pastime. He observed that if the government seeks action on a problem of social importance, it will act unilaterally and inform the public after the decision has been made, if at all. If it is indifferent to action, it will delegate a committee to study the issue and thereby conceal and obfuscate it from continued public attention. We have only to bring in again the earlier comparison between our two wars. Where is our domestic Tonkin resolution? Why don't we have an urban domino theory, which at least has empirical justification in Harlem, Detroit, and Washington? Reviewing the treatment of our racial and urban problems how wrong is it, how "dangerously incomplete," to view "the metropolitan problems almost solely in terms of race," to "devote our total attention to the debate of Black vs. White?" In other words, how groundless is this "unproductive paranoia" that we are admonished for?

The Future of the Metropolitan Political System

Lastly, we should examine the two questions proposed by Robert Wood for our consideration. The two are being stated as one:

Is this admittedly embryonic, evolving metropolitan political system—with many participants, without formal structure, dependent on federal money—strong enough to move fast enough to make a difference in the interlocked problems of the ghetto?

Applying our new focus on sincerity, we might ask, "Is this metropolitan system strong enough to first *admit* that there is a ghetto problem and confess its responsibility, as spokesmen of established, vested community interests, for the continuation of the problem?" Then, and only then, can we begin to get serious. It is moot twaddle to speak of "social justice" to a society that cherishes the memory and the progeny of its business bandits; that has routinized exploitation; and that has taken the hostile aggression of the economic predator and sublimated this into an almost religious constituent of our cultural ethic.

We must begin to understand certain things: the extent to which economic ideology and social ideology are interrelated in the cultural patterns recognized by the people of each society as "their way of life"; how each culture has drawn upon the construct of classic economic theory, extracting from it one of the three factors of production—land, labor, and capital—to emphasize in its social framework; how the communist scheme purports to revere labor, and how ours reveres capital, or property and money; and most importantly, we must understand that these ideologies are little more than the fabrications of idle men. The communists are not and never have been communists as defined by their ideology. We similarly, have never been capitalists, nor have we had a free economy, an open society, or social justice.

When you next hear of American social justice, remember John D. Rockefeller fuming, "the public be damned" or Charles (Bullmoose) Wilson's "what's good for General Motors is good for the country." Then this talk will fall in proper perspective.

We can continue this line by asking of the second part of the question, "What should cause the metropolitan system, which admittedly has caused 'gross inequities,' to deal with any urban blight?" This formulation contains an inherent contradiction of terms. To suggest that the middle class suburbs should assume their "metropolitan responsibilities" is to deny the dynamics of our society and the prescripts of our economic life that led the middle class to the suburbs. What responsibility do the suburbs have which will not be imposed on them? To think that all local subdivisions will rise voluntarily and recognize responsibility for the city that they worked to leave and forget, is visionary to an extreme.

If the metropolitan areas fail, the result will be, Robert Wood says, to "diminish the range of meaningful local government." Is this undesirable? Isn't a premise of his paper the harm already attributable to the existence of fragmentary government? Shouldn't we secretly hope, then, that the metropolitan area political structure fails utterly so that we can once and for all acknowledge that it is a moribund system unworthy of further effort? Abandonment might even reverse efforts in some quarters to dilute the growing not so subtle black power in American cities.

To close, it seems appropriate to share the title of a sermon which comes to mind as one ponders metropolitan politics. "Your actions resound so loud that I cannot hear what you say."

NOTE

1. Hodding Carter, "The Negro Exodus From the Delta Continues," *The New York Times Magazine,* March 10, 1968, p. 121.

COMMENTS: ROBERT C. WOOD

BECAUSE of differences in tone and emphasis, Dean Dumpson's presentation and mine seem at first reading to be far
apart. A closer reading, however, suggests that our rhetoric
exaggerated apparent differences and obscured substantial
agreements. We both clearly acknowledge:

that the pattern of metropolitan migration of the economically well-off from core city to suburb has been with us
throughout this century and earlier;

that the nonwhite urban poor today suffer special grievances
in this process which demand special remedies;

that despite the relative progress made economically and in
civil rights, aspirations for social justice remain properly
unabated;

that fragmented, divided, restrictive local urban governments
are poor instruments for reform.

Of course, there are differences in detail. I think Dean
Dumpson fails to distinguish between the Model Cities Program enacted in 1966 (and the *supplemental* funds it provides in addition to established Federal urban aid programs)
and the 1968 Omnibus Housing and Urban Development
Act, signed by the President on August 1. The first is a
demonstration program—sizable but still geared to cities willing to meet specific performance standards that sharply upgrade the quality of urban life. The second is a national
commitment to volume production—the construction of 6
million federally assisted housing units for poor and moderate-
income families in ten years at a rate ten times greater than
ever achieved before, effectively eliminating urban slums.

Details aside, our principal substantive difference is over the
impact and potential of the market economy in generating and

solving urban problems. At several places in his paper Dean Dumpson eloquently scores the shortcomings of the private sector in providing an acceptable urban environment. He refers to the past course of the American economy as "routinized exploitation" by "business bandits," and even now he believes the poor fare badly in the "resource-allocation" game. Yet, while condemning the consequences of classic economic theory, he proposes the same concept as a principal solution to social injustice and to the supplying of urban needs via an income maintenance program and bigger federal spending.

Fair enough. As I have indicated, bigger federal spending is already a fact—up three times in three years in urban aid programs alone—and destined to multiply even faster. Hopefully, too, an income maintenance program is close to reality although we need a more sophisticated version than any yet proposed to take into account regional and occupational variations.

But, given the past performance of the market mechanism in urban areas that Dean Dumpson identifies, I am not willing to embrace the simple injection of money as an exclusive response to urban ills, or to abandon the task of changing and strengthening public institutions, especially those at the local level. Six years of participation in the national government makes me less than sanguine that Washington can carry the total burden of urban reform or respond to the genuine cry for citizen participation in local affairs. Accordingly, I focus more strongly on devising common activities and emphasizing common purposes at the metropolitan level to enable a continental democracy to respond more flexibly and rapidly to the needs of its 200 million citizens.

But basically, Dean Dumpson and I remain together, I think. We are both determined that the pace of national assistance continue to expand; that new attention be given to the problems of migration and welfare; that an effective pattern of metropolitan social justice be realized—so that, to paraphrase his sermon title, our actions resound so loud, our words no longer need be heard.

6 CHARLES R. ADRIAN

The States and the Ghettos

Those of us who continue to see a meaningful task for state governments in an industrial–metropolitan society—some people are so unkind as to call us apologists for an anachronism—experience feelings of ambivalence. My own past writings show a wavering between cautious optimism concerning the future viability of the states and annoyed complaints that the states are sick.[1] In this paper, the potential for the states is measured against their ability to contribute toward the alleviation of the problems of the ghetto.

One need look at only two recent political events to see how severely the states are being tested. During the Detroit ghetto riot of 1967, both the Michigan National Guard and professional troops of the United States Army were used in attempts to restore order. Both local and national newspapers and news magazines made pointed references to the vastly inferior amateurs of the National Guard, calling them ill-trained, "trigger happy," "jumpy," unsympathetic toward the problems of the Negro poor, and generally incompetent. The Michigan National Guard can hardly be said to be a typical Guard outfit. Michigan state government has been among the state leaders for more than a generation, and it is reasonable to assume that its Guard is also one of the best—or perhaps, least incompetent.[2]

During the riots, the Michigan State Police were also called upon. This organization, by professional standards, is close to the top among state police forces. Yet, it was the most criticized of all law-enforcement units involved. Why? Probably because the state police had been preserved as a "lily white" outfit by a succession of police commissioners who had claimed that no qualified Negroes had applied for appointment as troopers. The organization, although well-trained technically, had come to symbolize white, middle class control over society.

A second symbolically important event took place in December, 1967, when the President signed a bill to extend federal minimum standards to all meat slaughtering and processing plants. For almost three generations, federal regulations had maintained the conditions under which meat was sold for human consumption at medically safe standards of quality. But the existing legislation applied only to about 85 percent of the meat products sold for human consumption—the remainder was prepared and sold within a single state and was not subject to federal legislation. Testimony before Congress indicated that some packing plants operated under filthy conditions by today's social and medical standards. The unsanitary and unsafe meat distributed by these unsupervised slaughter houses probably found its way disproportionately to the dinner tables of the poor in the ghettos. This seems likely because poor people use a disproportionate amount of the cheaper cuts and of processed meats (e.g., hamburger and wieners), the products whose quality and sanitation are most easily camouflaged. (Perhaps significantly, while 15 percent of all slaughtered meat was not subject to federal controls, about 25 percent of all processed meat was exempt.)

Why did the federal government take action to subject all meats intended for human consumption to federal standards? It was because the states—or at least nearly all states—had failed to provide their citizens with sufficient protection. They had been given at least sixty years in which to do so, and had failed.

The State in Historical Perspective

Traditionally, state governments have not been much concerned with urban problems, much less those of the urban

ghetto. Prior to the coming of the automobile two generations ago and the Great Depression one generation ago, state
governments had little direct contact with the ordinary citizen. They were concerned chiefly with the content of the
criminal and commercial law, the incarceration of criminals
and the mentally ill, and public higher education for the relatively few who went to college in those days. The states did
share decisions with national and local governments in the
pattern now called "cooperative federalism," but few functions were then performed by governments. And in the case
of those that were, the participation of the states was com-
monly the least visible.

The states were discouraged from expanding their urban
activities then, as they still are today, by urban political
leaders, who feared loss of control over local governments.
They were also inhibited by members of Congress and Presidents who did not want governors to seize credit for programs made possible by federal funds.

Actually, the traditional functions of state governments
provided them with possibilities for social reform that they
ignored. Their control over both criminal and commercial
law offered opportunities to deal with ghetto problems. Both
sets of laws, however, have always been designed to deal with
the concerns of the property-owning upper and middle classes
and have generally ignored both the values of the lower class
and the possibilities of being structured to aid members of
that class to advance economically. In these cases, as in
others that have been presented to state governments, such
as in their control over licensing of bars, hairdressers, and
barbers, they defaulted upon the opportunities afforded them.

Shortly before World War I, some of the states began to
respond to the demands of the "good roads movement" and
to provide for a state highway system. In this case, as in so
many cases before and since, many of the states did not move
until they were prodded by the federal government. The
federal-aid Highway Act of 1914 required a state to establish a highway department in order to be eligible for federal
aid. This spurred all the laggards into action.

The years of the Great Depression involved circumstances

that also brought state government closer to the ordinary citizen. During this period, the states were called upon to backstop for local governments in providing for public welfare needs in a time of acute unemployment. The states were reacting to the dire straits in which a broad cross-section of the general public found itself. Persons who had a few years earlier been relatively prosperous members of the working class or middle class found themselves bankrupt, desperate, and even starving. The condition existed in both urban and rural areas. The state governments acted to bail out bankrupt local governments. Then they, in turn, became dependent upon the federal government, the only institution with the resources necessary to meet the minimal needs of society in a time of great crisis.

During the years of World War II, state governments performed relatively unimportant functions and social issues were, at all levels of government, made subordinate to the war effort. After 1945, state governments continued to lack concern for the problems of an urban, industrial society. Only two areas of activity were exceptions. One was that of higher education, where the states began to react to demands for expanded public higher education facilities. Many of the states provided for vast increases in the numbers of students who could be accommodated at public institutions of higher learning. These changes were accomplished in a number of different ways. State universities were greatly expanded in size so as to permit a larger enrollment. State agricultural colleges were converted into universities. State teachers colleges became second echelon public universities, often with liberal arts, education, and business colleges. Municipal and poorly financed private institutions were taken over by the states. And systems of junior colleges were created or greatly expanded. The response in this area was primarily to middle class wants. Little concern was demonstrated for the intelligent but poor student, although a few governors proposed state scholarships based partly upon need and a very few trailblazing states provided for them. In a handful of cities, state aid was sought for new colleges to be located in ghettos.

The other area in which the states began to show leadership

was that of mental health. Beginning about 1948, state governors and gubernatorial candidates began to emphasize the need for mental health rehabilitation and the rejection of the earlier notion that mental patients need be given only minimal custodial care. In this case, unlike those relating to the newer programs in highways and higher education, the states did show concern for the problems of the poor in the urban ghettos. State government had expanded beyond the concerns of the middle class and the farmers. But this development was essentially fortuitous in character. The costs of care for the mentally ill and particularly the costs of rehabilitation were too great to be borne privately by middle class families. If care and treatment were to be provided by the state they would have to be made available to the mentally ill irrespective of class or income. (In the Deep South, however, segregation made it possible to withhold even this state service from the Negro poor.) The states have continued to encourage mental health facilities. A number of them today offer to pay more than one-half the cost of establishing new community mental health services.

During this period, states also began to increase their commitment toward the furthering of primary and secondary public education. To help relieve the strain on the general property tax, states began to offer grants-in-aid or shared taxes to local school districts for operating expenses or, in fewer cases, for capital outlays or the retirement of bond issues. Formulas for state educational aid were based to some extent upon considerations of the ability of the local district to raise funds within its own area, but they did not take into account the special needs and problems of the most poverty-ridden areas of the countryside or the urban ghetto. Congressional action in the school-aid act of 1967 contrasts sharply with the action taken in most states. Most of the money (60 percent) authorized by Congress for appropriation was to be used for educational improvement in rural and urban ghettos. These areas would also benefit from other· provisions of the act, including programs to prevent dropouts and to aid in adult education. This act followed the general pattern for slum education established in the Economic Opportunity

Act of 1964 (the antipoverty act) and the Elementary and Secondary Education Act of 1965.

Outside the areas of highways, education, and mental health, the great majority of the states did very little, and for some functions, almost nothing in the generation following World War II to help meet the problems of a rapidly growing urban society. Least of all did state governments concern themselves with the urban ghetto. Mass transportation, public housing, urban renewal, tenement health and safety standards, professional-quality police protection, and medical services for the poor were concerns of almost no state governments. Even today, after much publicity concerning these problems, the pattern is largely unchanged. State agencies, such as departments of urban affairs, are being created, but they are not—up to the present at least—being financed at a level that would make their presence felt in dealing with ghetto social problems.

Poverty and the States

In the 1950s and early 1960s, a few of the more prosperous but problem-ridden industrial states began to become concerned with urban poverty. (New York was unique in the extent of its efforts in this respect.) A very few began to become concerned with problems of public transportation, outpatient mental health facilities in slum areas, public housing, and the promotion of job opportunities for low-skilled slum dwellers. Most of the urban industrial states also began to pay some attention to civil rights starting in the 1950s. Fair employment practices acts with commissions to carry out their provisions, open housing, and public accommodations laws were widely adopted. By the mid-1960s an examination of state legal codes revealed that there was some recognition and concern about the fact that America had become an urban industrial nation. But there was almost nothing to show that in most of the states, urban areas contained a ghetto with a hard-core poor population, confronted with special problems virtually unknown to the middle class or even to those in the working class who were employed more or less regularly in industrial jobs with wages that were negotiated by the professional representatives of labor unions.

In the 1960s, Presidents Kennedy and Johnson began to emphasize the need for governmental action relative to the problems of the poor. Their proposals, together with the writings of Michael Harrington and others, served to emphasize the great cost involved in meeting the problems of an urban, industrial society and particularly in caring for the marginal members of that society, persons who could not compete because of educational, psychological, or discriminatory handicaps. State governments, faced with the high cost of meeting these problems, once again largely failed when challenged. In the mid-1960s, a number of conservative governors were elected to join with the ordinarily conservative state legislative majorities. These governors generally ignored the problems of the urban ghetto or denied that they were a state responsibility, or, in some cases, that they were a responsibility of government of any kind, but rather should be met and overcome in the traditional American pattern of individual incentive and effort. State governors, who had in the past always been oriented toward the yeoman farmer and the urban middle class citizen, emphasized not solutions to urban problems, but the desirability of economy and the avoidance of the kinds of tax increases that would be necessary if ghetto problems were to be taken seriously and efforts made to deal with them. Similarly, governors reacted to summer riots in urban ghettos by demanding not legislation that would aid in eliminating the causes of such riots, but legislation that was punitive in character, serving to treat the symptom rather than the cause by providing for harsher punishments for law violators.

When Governor Ronald Reagan took office in California in 1967, one of his first acts was to close many of the ghetto service centers which had been established to permit slum residents to learn about available governmental services in a single government office and to reduce the threat and confusion involved when a poorly educated and desperate individual is sent from one governmental agency to another. Reagan explained the closings in terms of an economy move in the face of desperate financial problems. It seems more likely, however, that his principal objection was to the spending of state tax money upon the urban poor. These centers had been established in order to decrease information costs and increase the efficiency of service to the needy. Such a goal was however, for Reagan, dysfunctional. Consistent with this attitude, Reagan in 1967 vetoed bills to aid the gifted children of poor families and to provide college education grants to children in poverty areas. By item veto, he also reduced by one-third an item to finance the special training of teachers for the children of the poor.

In Florida, in early 1968, Governor Claude Kirk offered his strong personal support to a proposal by the Miami Chief of Police to deal harshly with Negro slum hoodlums. It was a proposal, once again, to deal with the symptom, the individual criminal product of the slum, rather than the cause, the social conditions that produce and perpetuate the ghetto. Six weeks after the "crackdown," crime in the Miami ghetto had been sharply reduced, but the policy also appeared to have had a negative effect upon race relations in the city.[3] The effect on race relations gave promise to be more lasting than was the reduction in the incidence of crime. Kirk offered no program for a positive approach to the basic causes.

With friends such as these state governments surely have no need for enemies.

The Potential for State Action

The areas in which the state government could assist in improving conditions in the ghetto are many. They include:

The police. City police have come to symbolize the repression of the poor. At least, this is so in the minds of some slum dwellers and in the way ghetto problems are sometimes presented by cartoonists and editorial writers. Empirical evidence, however, indicates that the typical slum dweller wants effective, courteous police protection just as does the middle class suburbanite.[4] Although many cases of illegal force being used by the police undoubtedly have taken place,[5] the popular expression of misuse ("Police brutality!") appears to be more a slogan and symbol for the more extreme ghetto activists than a concern of typical ghetto citizens. Even so, one of the great urban needs of today is for a police force equipped educationally and psychologically to deal with the alienated, frustrated, poorly informed slum dweller. In past generations, a policeman needed only to be strong, brave, and devoted to the respect of middle class values. The level of his educational achievement was largely irrelevant, even up to the office of chief. Today, the work situation of the policeman is very different. Whatever his personal beliefs may be, he is not qualified for his job unless he is willing to apply the same standards of enforcement in the ghetto as he does in middle class areas of the city. He must know (even if he cannot approve) the current rules governing civil rights and liberties. And he must be more a diplomat and negotiator than a user of sanctions.

What police departments need today is better educated, trained, and paid personnel. But while the policeman's job has recently become more important, it has also become less attractive. Cities and counties are going to require a great deal of assistance, both financially and in the provision of training facilities, if they are to furnish qualified police forces to the next generation. What is needed are massive programs for the training and in-service retraining of policemen. And these need to be supplemented by grants-in-aid that will enable cities to hire and retain police of sufficient quality. In a few cases, state governments may be willing and able to meet this need; in most areas of the nation, police training and financial subsidization will probably have to be a function of the national government.

The administration of justice. States, while seeking to maintain a community-wide, or classless, set of goals for justice, might well concentrate upon the ways by which the administration of justice for the poor—in regard to sentencing, parole, and probation—might more closely resemble that for the prosperous. Several states are now working on this. They are experimenting with an approach, originated in New York, by which even poor persons (with reasonably good police records) may be released on their own recognizance rather than being held in jail for weeks or months in lieu of bond. Some states are also experimenting with the use of the old Wisconsin work-release programs for more serious offenders. This plan, originated in 1913 and used subsequently in numerous states, was until recently used only for minor violators. It permitted convicts to take jobs in the community or visit relatives on weekends, but required them to return to jail on weekday nights. Experiments to date offer considerable hope. Some states are also encouraging, through grants, the use of community residential centers, or "halfway houses," which can shelter the released convict while he strives to regain a useful place and acceptance in a community.

Public rapid transit. Slum dwellers often cannot afford automobiles but they need means by which to move within reasonable levels of convenience to areas where employment exists. Public transportation is logically the answer but such transportation must be subsidized by some level of government. Local governments are generally in no position to afford either to build a new rapid transit system or to subsidize its continuing operation. Because middle and upper income persons have one or more automobiles, it seems unrealistic to expect that in the future mass transportation systems can be developed without subsidy. Either the state or federal governments could provide such a subsidy. The pervasive apathy of nearly all state legislatures and many governors gives us a good indication as to where the assistance is likely to come from.

Public assisted housing. State financed public housing is another area for possible action. In the 1930s, the New York legislature and governor became interested in housing needs and they have from that time to the present been concerned at least to some degree with meeting slum housing problems. The other states have done practically nothing. They have usually not even attempted to adopt and enforce modern and effective laws for safe and sanitary housing. Some governors have made recommendations to legislatures for meaningful action to overcome the slovenly approaches of many cities to minimum housing standards, but these have generally been ignored. A few states have attempted in recent years to aid in slum removal through redevelopment plans aimed at replacing substandard housing with job-creating industries and business. But the states are probably not financially able to underwrite the costs of guaranteeing mortgages that would permit low-income persons to buy homes or condominium apartments. Except in a few of the richest states, only the national government can be expected to do that.

Urban renewal. The states, similarly, have done little or nothing relative to urban renewal, except perhaps to petition Congress to give them a larger voice in policy making. Few states have done anything to help with the critical problems of financing and minimum standards. They have tended to ignore the latter and to rely upon the federal government for the former.

Health and hospitals. In the areas of public health and hospitals, little has been done to help overcome some of the major slum problems. As is usually the case, the state has acted only where the broad interests of society at large coincide with those of the slum dwellers. Hence, the relatively high rates of venereal disease and of tuberculosis in slum areas have resulted in state programs of significance—often inspired by federal aid, however.

Mental health. Mental health programs, too, have aided ghetto dwellers. Many states have established effective outpatient clinics and halfway houses that have been beneficial to the poor. Some studies have shown that mental illness is particularly to be found in the ghetto, indicative that provision for care and rehabilitation in that area is especially important. Social workers have probably been particularly effective in providing some assistance to the mentally ill, having been able to refer cases to the appropriate treatment centers. Large numbers of needy slum dwellers, however, are apparently never referred to mental-health treatment centers, and state facilities generally are not concentrated in the densely populated, problem-ridden slum.

Welfare. In the field of welfare, the federal government has now dominated policy-making for well over a generation, and it would be unrealistic to expect leadership relative to over-all policy to come from any other source. Support levels for those on welfare differ considerably from one state to another, and some innovations have taken place at the state level. But we do not find state leaders making imaginative suggestions to Congress and to the President for revisions in today's outmoded approaches to welfare—approaches that were designed to meet the particular problems of the depression era. The state legislatures have done little or nothing innovative concerning the problems of slum welfare recipients, even though recommendations have come to them steadily from professional social workers, from economists, and from many others. They have done little, for example, to ameliorate the problems of the aged, thus the elderly poor continue to live in slums where they pay disproportionately high prices for food and shelter.

One of the major points of friction in the welfare system in recent years has been the question of the family with no father and with the children possibly illegitimate. Aid to· dependent children has been criticized—and widely publicized—as a program that rewards immorality and shiftlessness. State leaders have been quick to make charges relative to this kind of situation, yet they have done little to try to do more than punish the runaway father or the mother on welfare who has another child out of wedlock. Abandoned mothers with several children living at home have often pointed out that if a few relatively inexpensive services were available, they would be willing to go to work and probably could take themselves off the welfare roles and make contributions to the nation's economy. Yet, no matter how belatedly, it was the national government rather than the states that acted to provide for such facilities as subsidized day-care centers, located in the ghettos, designed to free the mother to take a job and support her family if she believes she is in a position to do so. (A change in policy to permit the mother of young children to work had to be made by the federal government, to be sure. The important point is that the incentive for change came from the U.S. Bureau of the Budget, not from state agencies.)

Parks and recreation. Parks and recreation facilities on a no-charge or low-cost basis are particularly needed in the ghetto. The states have, however, generally ignored these needs and have either offered no excuse or have suggested that responsibility for parks and recreation of this sort rests with local governments. State facilities are generally located many miles —perhaps half a day's travel—from slum areas. They have been designed principally for the benefit of the more prosperous members of the working class and members of the middle class. Most state facilities are designed on the assumption that their users will possess their own automobile and perhaps also a camper or camping equipment and that the users will have the necessary funds to buy an admission and perhaps also a camping permit. Both state and local governments continue to design recreation facilities with the average or near-average income person in mind. They are not intended for the use of marginal members of society. The wealthy go to private resorts and the slum-dweller is still expected to provide for his idle time on his own, as was the case a century ago. Only a few states have seriously considered expending funds for recreation facilities located directly within ghetto areas.

The National Guard. Because of its importance in times of civil disorder, this is one of the most significant state government functions that relate to the ghetto. The Guard has been used in nearly all of the ghetto riots of the 1960s.[6] In each of these cases, its use became the center of conflict, often very heated conflict. Indeed, conflict has surrounded the activities of the Guard throughout the American industrial era.[7] The Guard has received praise and has been welcomed when it has been used for search and rescue purposes, as in cases of forest fires, floods, earthquakes, or hurricanes. But most of the time it has been seen as an instrument for the repression of the underprivileged. During the 1920s and 1930s and even before, it was often used in strikes, usually on the side of management and the strike breakers.

In case of ghetto riots, the first effort to restore order is usually made by local police. Next, the state police or highway patrol is usually requested. The National Guard is called in when a situation seems to be getting genuinely out of control. Only in rare cases will the mayor of a large city or the governor of the state concede that he cannot handle the situation and ask for federal troops. It is probably not in the office-holder's political interest to admit inability to control.

The National Guard has generally performed poorly in riot control. The reason is clear enough. It consists mainly of amateurs, aided by a few semi-professionals. These men are sent to do a job that, even in the hands of professionals, is not easy to accomplish successfully. To make matters worse, the Guard consists largely of persons out of upper working-class and lower middle class white families where distrust of and discrimination against Negroes are particularly likely to exist.

Something needs to be done concerning both the National Guard and riot control. The Guard is probably the greatest waste of taxpayer money of any state government operation. (The money comes largely from the federal government, but it is still taxpayer money.) It so happens, however, that the Guard is supported by extremely powerful interest groups and has been able to resist all pressures for change that are not internally approved. At the present time, rather than concentrating upon improving itself (although it is making some few efforts in this direction) it is seeking a better image through public relations activities. In addition to the "patriotic" forces that support the Guard, it enjoys support from the pervasive American ideology which holds that the federal government should not become involved in anything that could be handled at the state or local levels.

The most rational approach to the controlling of ghetto riots would involve two principles. One would be to minimize the activities of the local police or the state police in any riot area. The image of the police has become less favorable in recent years as urban conflict levels have risen and its legitimacy as an instrument of social control has increasingly been questioned. The police would probably find greater acceptance if they did not have to engage in riot control. The second principle is that riot control should be made the responsibility of professionals. The police in large cities are generally professional enough, and so are many of the state police and highway patrolmen. But if these groups are not to be used for the reasons just given, we are just about left with the use of Federal Military Police and Special Forces personnel. If ideology prevails over rationality, however, then the only alternative would seem to be a sharp upgrading of selected units of National Guards with frequent training, proper equipment, and an understanding that they will be used specifically for riot-control purposes.

The question of what to do to minimize future ghetto riots lies squarely in the laps of state governors and legislators. At the moment, they do not appear to be doing very much about the problem. Characteristically, however, the federal government is. In the fall of 1967, the United States Army sent teams to the nation's larger cities to develop a riot-control plan in each city. According to the *New York Times:*

The teams are under instructions to put together thick folders of information on each of scores of potentially explosive cities. The data will include street maps, aerial photos, and details on communication nets and proposed command posts and emergency camp sites.

The teams will also try to determine in advance the lines of responsibility for military units, local and state police units and National Guard units. . . .

"There always has been and will continue to be a great reluctance to deploy Federal troops," one defense official said, "and we think the Governors and Mayors will try to insure that their forces will be trained to handle disorders because they don't want Federal troops either."[8]

A Program of Improvement

What the states ought to be concentrating on today is a set of programs of their own, designed to supplement and raise the level of services that currently exist largely as the result of Federal innovation and financing. They should concentrate on opening up areas of opportunity for the poor. Action here should probably center at first on the adoption and strengthening of fair employment practices and open-housing legislation in order to permit further progress in seeking equality. Some of the states have done a relatively good job on employment although most of the state commissions are very weak so far as powers of seeking compliance are concerned. They have made little headway on open housing, although progress has not been completely lacking and in many cases the states have authorized local governments to adopt open-housing ordinances. Beyond encouraging equal treatment for all in employment, housing, and public accommodations, the states ought to concentrate on providing special educational programs for those living in ghetto areas. The federal antipoverty program is doing something in this connection, but more legislation of the type vetoed by the Governor in California last year is needed. The states, after all, have the fundamental responsibility for education and they have long supported special education or other educational programs, such as those for the blind or deaf, vocational agricultural education, and the subsidy of returning veterans who resume their education.

The states could also well be involved very deeply in areas where they are currently doing little or nothing. These include mass transportation; urban renewal and the elimination of urban blight generally; the provision of low-cost housing, enabling slum clearance without creating new slums with no improvement over the *status quo ante* and with the slum dweller merely paying higher rents; mental-health rehabilitation facilities on an outpatient basis in slum areas; and recreation facilities in those areas where recreation is most badly needed and the danger of antisocial idle-time activities is the greatest in its absence. Public and private recreational facilities are today widely available to members of the middle class but not to the poor.

Finally, state leaders might be just as active as our leaders in the federal government and in the social work profession in seeking more modern and more efficacious means by which to provide for public welfare aid where needed. This planning, of course, should take place within the context of the probable future demands of the system. It should consider a future in which automation will become increasingly important in industrial production, the work week will be shortened, and the person with no skills or very low skills will be increasingly less relevant to the American system of production.

98]   CHARLES R. ADRIAN

The Credibility Canyon

The states have serious problems in attempting to improve their image and to meet the changing needs of society. Most of them have not yet earned the confidence of the leaders of organized labor. Liberals have been notoriously hostile toward state governments, arguing that they are anachronisms which should be ignored if they cannot actually be eliminated altogether. The states, even putting aside these kinds of problems, do not have the sound tax base or control of their credit that the federal government possesses. They have had difficulties in raising the funds necessary simply to keep up with existing program levels, much less to finance new programs that result from the emerging problems of metropolitan America. And even with modest goals, state debt and tax levels have increased much faster than have their federal equivalents in the last generation.[9]

The states have not done well in reducing their credibility gap. Only in a sprinkling of situations have they shown that they can deal with emerging problems on their own or as the leader in a team approach involving two or more levels of government. State-sponsored reports about problems often conclude by urging the federal government to supply more money while at the same time permitting the states to have greater control over its use. Since the fiddler usually does call the tune and since professional administrators are much more likely to be found at the national than at the state level, these kinds of suggestions are not likely to bolster an image of state government as a viable institution. Indeed, the suggestions sometimes sound like whining pleas.

Even California, which has long prided itself on being a leader among states and able to meet many of its problems by itself, does not always come off too well in respect to its urban responsibilities in comparison with those of the federal government. We see this, for example, in a report called, *Recommended Roles for California State Government in Federal Urban Programs*. This was a report of the Inter-Governmental Council on Urban Growth. The Council is headed by a distinguished urban planner, William L. C.

Wheaton, but it is dominated by state and local officials. The principal recommendations of the Council were three:

1. California should actively seek the adoption of federal programs for federal-state tax credits and the loosening of categorical restrictions on grant-in-aid to state and local government.

2. The state government, together with representatives of local governments, should participate aggressively in the design, drafting and processing of federal grant programs.

3. There should be created in the Governor's office a Secretary for Urban Affairs.

For such a major area of concern, these are relatively weak recommendations. They once again call for continued federal tax sharing but with greater state-level control. California and a few other states have a professional bureaucracy qualified to develop and administer programs and have personnel in the bureaucracy that is able to hold its own with counterparts in the Federal bureaucracy. But this is not the situation in the great majority of our states, even including a number of highly industrialized states, such as Indiana, Ohio, Pennsylvania, and Texas.

The Ghetto Tomorrow

We might look briefly at the future of the ghetto. The best hope for those who today live in ghettos—assuming that they would prefer not to—is to look at what happened to the ghetto dwellers of the past. Much of the incentive for outward or upward movement must come from those who now live there just as has been the case in the past. Their task is more difficult today than it formerly was, however, and for many reasons. The low-skilled industrial job, the small street-corner business, and the reasonably well-paying industrial job available to the unskilled, poorly educated person are no longer much of a reality. Different patterns for job advancement must be developed. In addition to this, of course, the ghetto dweller is today most probably either a Negro, a Mexican-American, or a Puerto Rican and his chance for assimilation, economically, culturally, and socially, is much less than was that of the Irish,

Italian, German, or Slav. His chances of advancement without government aid are much less than they were for the urban ghetto dweller of a generation or two ago.

In the past, the route upward from the ghetto has never been easy to find or climb, but it has never been closed. There is reason for concern today because the route is more difficult than ever and the things that need to be done to keep the road open are of a different kind from those needed in the past. This latter fact still is not recognized by many of our national and state leaders. Still, things are being done by the federal poverty program, inadequate as it is, and by a few of the states. There are still opportunities for advancement in the traditional American manner, of course. The ambitious son of the ghetto can still open the most traditional exits, those provided by entering into the clergy, organized crime, professional sports, popular entertainment, or politics. Even the confused tragedy of Vietnam offers opportunity; for those who survive and suffer no permanent disabling psychological or physical wounds will return to heavily subsidized education programs, and education is today, in contrast to the past, the best single route to the outside.

The most likely ghetto developments in the coming decades will involve a continued removal from the ghetto of the most talented and highly motivated individuals. In the future as in the past these are likely to be the ones who will find the pathway leading to middle class suburbia. Once the upwardly mobile Negroes, Mexican-Americans, and Puerto Ricans have left, there probably will be more low-status, highly unskilled large groups to take over the ghetto. Eventually, it will no longer be occupied by those who are discriminated against because of race, color, creed, life style, language, accent, or dialect. Instead, it will be the dwelling place of the psychologically, physiologically, and mentally handicapped. A complex society will always have a considerable number of people who are unable to compete effectively under the established rules of the day. These people will be the responsibilities of government at all levels and the way in which we treat them may be the best test yet of our real attitudes toward our fellow man.

Conclusion

The weaknesses of the states can be summarized as follows:

1. The states cannot do much to influence the over-all economic pattern of the nation. The role of job creator must be played by the federal and local governments most of the time. Only Washington, acting with private business and industry, has the power to shape the job market in terms of size and types of skills. Only local leaders can seek to attract jobs to particular communities.

2. The states are ill equipped to act in concert. They are jealous of one another, and compete for job-creating industries and in seeking to keep taxes low. Often only federal action makes state action possible, as in the case of unemployment compensation laws in the 1930s.

3. Only about six states—perhaps ten if we are generous—can be said to have fully professional bureaucracies manning all agencies. (Social welfare is professionalized, in most states, only because of federal insistence.) Increasingly, only the professionals in a given field can cope with complex modern functions. When the states lack the necessary personnel, only the local or national governments can act if the problem cannot be handled satisfactorily in the private sector.

4. The marginal cost of adding a new program or raising the standards of an existing one are higher at the state level than at the national. This is so because the national government has the more powerful tax base and one that, despite outcries of protest, can raise large amounts of money quite easily, largely because of its claim to priority in the use of the sharply graduated income tax. It also can borrow money more cheaply than can the states and essentially controls its own credit structure, along with that of the entire nation. The states have no similar advantage.

5. The states are largely invisible, noninnovative political structures. Indeed, their leaders seem to have a defeatist attitude and an inferiority feeling when comparing themselves with the federal government. This syndrome may be related to the general inferiority of the states' bureaucracies. It is true that Max Weber seemed to argue the opposite, that mature

bureaucracies are noninnovative, but this is true only within limits. They certainly do resist change when someone seeks to impose it from the outside. They have their own values, standards, goals, and procedures and will not willingly (or consciously) change them. But they do urge the development of public policies that meet their professional standards, and it is this type of innovation that is largely missing in the states with amateur, jerry-built bureaucracies.

6. The typical citizen pays least attention to state government activities, including elections to fill its offices. He trusts state governments less than either national or local governments and he expects the least from them of all American governments.

The states are weak, but they are not without resources. They possess legitimacy. It is relatively a weak sense of legitimacy, but it exists. The states are accepted as having a regular place in the American political system and their general political behavior is quite widely known. It is roughly predictable and hence does not, to most interested citizens, loom as a threat.

A particular resource of the states is the high degree to which they are accepted and trusted by conservatives. Conservatives are attracted to the states in part because of the weaknesses listed above, of course. But the allegiance is broader than that and it offers a basis for potential involvement of the states in governmental activity of all types.

Finally, state governments are in a strong position to adjust federal programs to fit local values and expectations. Such adjustments are not necessarily viewed as desirable by all, for they may inhibit or limit federal plans so as to fit parochial views of the desirable, including the desirable in race relations. But even when citizens of the nation as a whole do not approve of action in a particular state, such action may help make the system viable by modifying parochial behavior toward the national norm.

In summary, we can say that the states have a part to play in dealing with the problems of the ghetto. It is a relatively small expanding part and is not likely to include much of the critically important function of innovation. Instead, the states will, for the most part, be involved in cooperative efforts to deal with these problems. They will assume a portion of the cost of financing programs and will help focus activities by honing national policies to fit regional conditions.

Most innovation and the bulk of the financing of programs in the ghetto will have to come from the national government. The second largest portion will be from local governments. But even though the states will—as usual—bring up the rear, their involvement will be significant in terms of partial financing, refinement of policy, and even occasionally in the development of supplemental programs. The effort of the states is and will be considerable when judged by the number of dollars and persons involved, but it is and will continue to be dwarfed by the magnitude of the problems we face.

NOTES

1. Cf. Charles R. Adrian, "State and Local Government Participation in the Design and Administration of Intergovernmental Programs," *Annals of the American Academy of Political and Social Science,* 359 (May 1965), 35–43; and Charles Press and Charles R. Adrian, "Why Our State Governments Are Sick," *Antioch Review,* 24 (Summer 1964), 149–165.

2. See the *Detroit News* and *Detroit Free Press* for July and August 1967. See also *The New York Times, Time,* and *Newsweek* for the period. The Detroit riot began on July 23, 1967.

3. *The New York Times,* February 19, 1968.

4. John F. Kraft, *Attitudes of Negroes in Various Cities* (New York: John F. Kraft, Inc., 1966).

5. Ed Cray, *The Big Blue Line* (New York: Coward-McCann, 1967). Cray is a staff member of the American Civil Liberties Union.

6. For the Watts riot, see Jerry Cohen and William S. Murphy, *Burn, Baby, Burn!* (New York: Dutton, 1966); for those of 1967, see National Advisory Commission on Civil Disorders, *Report,* 1968.

7. See Bennett M. Rich and Philip H. Burch, Jr., "The Changing Role of the National Guard," *American Political Science Review,* 50 (September 1956), 702–706; William H. Riker, *Soldiers of the States* (Washington, D.C.: Public Affairs Press, 1957).

8. *The New York Times,* November 23, 1967.

9. Frederick C. Mosher and Orville F. Poland, *The Costs of American Government* (New York: Dodd, Mead, 1964).

7 | DANIEL J. ELAZAR

The Outlook for
Creative Federalism

The rapid changes taking place in American politics in the 1960s are nowhere better illustrated than in the shift of political concern among progressives from an overriding commitment to greater centralization of power in Washington to demands for radical decentralization even at the local level. This shift is variously motivated and differently manifested among several segments of the articulate population of the United States. It is reflected in such varied concerns as the drive for "creative federalism" and the advocacy of "neighborhood self-government."

The argument for creative federalism represents the position of the national administration and, though clearly decentralist in tone, is almost conservative in its attempts to legitimize heavy federal involvement in the domestic government of the country.[1] The argument for neighborhood self-government is most frequently voiced by that rather amorphous aggregation of "post-liberal" reformers—including students and Negroes—often known as the "New Left" in opposition to what they believe to be too much outside interference in decisions that vitally affect residents of urban ghettos and in line with their general commitment to the creation of meaningful community within mass society.[2]

The relative positions of the Washington-oriented liberals on the one hand, and the New Left, on the other, may well indicate that we are coming to the point where history enters into another one of its curious twists, whereby defenders of "big government" and national planning *per se* will be the conservatives while those seeking change will be increasingly in favor of localizing power. What is significant about both positions today, however, is their common source: the American propensity for—one might well say commitment to—the principles, processes, and spirit of federalism.

The Meaning of Federal Democracy

In strictly governmental terms, federalism is a form of political organization which unites separate polities within an overarching political system so that all maintain their fundamental political integrity, distributing power among general and constituent governments so that they all share in the system's decision-making and executing powers.[3] In a larger sense, federalism represents the linking of free men and their communities through lasting but limited political arrangements to protect certain rights and achieve specific common ends while preserving their respective integrities.

Federal democracy is the authentic American contribution to democratic thought and republican government. Stemming in part from the constitutional ideas of the English "natural rights" school of the seventeenth and early eighteenth centuries, the American political synthesis that created federal democracy drew as much or more from the Puritan idea of the covenant relationship, through which they believed all proper human society was organized.[4] The covenant idea (the Latin root of the word "federal" means *covenant* or compact) demands a different kind of political relationship (and perhaps, in the long run, a different kind of human relationship) than that emphasized by theories of mass democracy of the kind that have attracted many adherents since the French Revolution; one that emphasizes partnership between individuals, groups, and governments in the pursuit of justice; cooperative relationships that make the partnership real; and negotiation among the partners as the basis for sharing power. The political history of the United

States can be read as an illustrative commentary on that idea.

In its most practical manifestations, the workings of American federalism are reflected in the hard political processes of cooperation and bargaining which inform the system's mosaic of governments and interests so that all those who can demonstrate that they are entitled to sit in on the great game of government can share in the development and implementation of public policies affecting them. Thus when we speak of federal democracy in America we are not simply talking about convenient political arrangements that should be maintained because we are accustomed to them (which is frequently the conservative view) or administrative decentralization that is valuable because it gets things done (which is the view frequently heard from the spokesmen of the present national administration). We are talking about a comprehensive pattern of political organization that permeates every aspect of American political life, shaping governments and organized interests alike and affecting every governmental process from party politics to desegregation. It is a pattern based on three great, if implicit, political principles which have developed out of the realities of American political life and which reenforce the patterns of American political behavior at every turn: *contractual noncentralization, territorial democracy*, and *multifaceted partnership*.

Contractual noncentralization—the structured dispersion of power among many centers whose legitimate authority is constitutionally guaranteed—is the key to the widespread and entrenched diffusion of power that remains the principal characteristic of and argument for federal democracy. Noncentralization is not the same as decentralization, though the latter term is frequently—and erroneously—used in its place to describe the American system. Decentralization implies the existence of a central authority, a central government. The government that can decentralize can recentralize if it so desires, hence in decentralized systems the diffusion of power is actually a matter of grace, not right and, in the long run, is usually treated as such as the British experience reveals.[5]

In a noncentralized political system power is so diffused that it cannot be legitimately centralized or concentrated without breaking the structure and spirit of the constitution. The United States has such a noncentralized system. We have a national—or general—government which functions powerfully in many areas for many purposes but not a central government controlling all the lines of political communication and decision-making. Our states are not creatures of the federal government but, like the latter, derive their authority directly from the people. Structurally, they are substantially immune from federal interference. Functionally, they share many activities with the federal government but without forfeiting their policy-making roles and decision-making powers.

In the language of contemporary social science, centralization and decentralization are extremes of the same continuum while noncentralization represents another phenomenon altogether. In systems located on the former continuum, it is rather simple to measure the flow of power one way or another. In noncentralized systems, however, it is a considerably more difficult matter. Simple evidence of national government involvement tells us little or nothing about the relative strength of the various power centers in policy-making, administration, or what have you. Is social welfare policy really made in Washington because Congress provides a major share of the funds for certain program categories through grants-in-aid? The evidence has it that it is not.[6] The primary diffusion of power makes "involvement" take on many different meanings. Even apparently unilateral programs may be substantially shaped by the other governments through the political process and as those in the social welfare area know, the amount of money spent is no indication of the degree of political control exercised.

To use different imagery, decentralization implies hierarchy—a pyramid of governments with gradations of power flowing down from the top. The imagery of hierarchy has become the dominant one in American political discussion today, but it is a misleading one. Noncentralization describes a matrix of governments with powers so distributed that the rank order of the several governments is not fixed—e.g., if the national government is primary in the field of foreign affairs, the states are primary in the fields of highways and higher education, and the localities primary in matters of elementary education and zoning. The source of funding may affect the ordering of governments relative to particular functions but rarely alters the order significantly.

Because these principles are the products of political realities, they have important and immediate practical consequences which lead to the primary operational fact of the American system: the necessity to involve all planes of government in virtually every activity of government in such a way as to give each an irrevocable share of the decision-making and executing processes. Thus, the basic noncentralized relationship between the federal government and the states has been extended, *de facto,* through the political process to the localities as well. Even though the localities remain theoretically the creatures of their states, in fact they have gained a substantial measure of entrenched political power because they have been able to capitalize on the spirit of noncentralization—the spirit of federalism, if you will—in their day-to-day operations and in their bargaining with other governments.

Noncentralization makes it possible for local governments to develop policies and programs of their own within a system that is too complex to allow them the luxury of isolation; to acquire outside aids for carrying out those policies and programs and adapt those aids to their own needs. They are usually encouraged to do so by state and federal authorities but they do so even if they are not.

Noncentralization in the United States is based on territorial divisions, from states to precincts. The permanent boundaries of the former and the well-nigh permanent boundaries of their major subdivisions serve as strong bulwarks for the diffusion of power. As permanent boundaries, they offer continued opportunities for diverse interests to exercise power without fear of retribution from "higher authority" while, possessing the neutrality of so-called artificial boundaries, they prevent the confinement of power to a few select interests. Because every interest, new or old, is located willy-nilly in some formally defined political territory, every interest can gain some measure of expression more or less proportional to its strength, simply by making use of the country's political mechanisms.

Territorial democracy also shapes the organization of virtually all domestic government activity. In truth, most welfare programs are not national at all even when they are nationally funded. With the exception of Old Age and Survivors' Insurance and the veterans' services, all federal social welfare programs are tied to the system of territorial democracy to a greater or lesser degree. They are established, organized and administered by the states or their local subdivisions. Even Medicare relies upon the states for certification of hospitals and other such functions while most of the major health and welfare programs are state-centered. Federal funds make those welfare programs possible and, as a consequence, give Congress and the federal administration a "license" to bargain for national policies. The states—still the keystones in the American governmental arch—remain the custodians of the American social welfare system and the localities remain the basic distributors of public welfare resources.[7] Even the Office of Economic Opportunity, which attempted to break through the established systems of welfare politics, had to take cognizance of these truths. Its efforts to bypass the state and local governments have contributed to the emasculation of its projects without succeeding in preventing the intervention of the duly constituted officials.

Noncentralization and territorial democracy are made operationally effective by the intergovernmental and public-private partnership that has grown up within the framework of the Constitution. This partnership is based on the well-nigh universal sharing of functions which has already been mentioned. Sharing involves a whole complex of deep seated governmental and extragovernmental arrangements designed to recognize and accommodate national and local interests and preserve the basic integrities of the several governments that participate in the system, while mobilizing sufficient energy to maintain and develop positive public programs.[8]

Intergovernmental sharing is necessary because the dynamic character of American society spreads virtually all issues and demands throughout the governmental system, preventing any easy isolation of particular governments or communities. It is possible because more interests are shared by the several planes of government than not, confining conflict to questions of means rather than ends. This does not mean that conflict is insignificant but that it remains limited and, hence, manageable. All this has been substantially true even in the case of the civil rights issue, for some states the rare exception to the general rule. While, for the whites in power in certain Southern states, there is a state-federal disagreement over national ends, those states are in the minority. Over three-fifths of the states are at least in agreement with federal civil rights policies and many of them are further ahead.

Sharing is effectuated through cooperative action based on continuing negotiation among institutions and close interpersonal relations among their representatives. The negotiations are open to all who can pay the ante to sit in on the game. Thus federal grants in the social welfare and other fields become bases for negotiation with the states and localities rather than firm demands for particular policies, ways to crystallize and reflect nationwide trends rather than means for imposing fixed national patterns. Implementation of America's social welfare programs at a more or less uniform level across the country relies heavily on the existence of the social welfare professions and the spread of social welfare professionals through the literally thousands of separate welfare jurisdictions. The sharing relationships developed among these professionals, no matter what governments they happen to be serving, are of crucial importance in effecting these cooperative programs. The same professionals, through their associations, are heavily involved in shaping the programs and drawing up the guidelines they implement.

These principles of noncentralization, territorial democracy, and partnership permeate every aspect of the American political system. They are not simply features of grant-in-aid programs or intergovernmental consultations. Their influence is felt in the party system, in the administration of so-called direct federal functions in the organization of our national defense and even in the realm of foreign affairs. Through them, the full implications of the federal bargain that unites peoples and polities are made meaningful in the arena where political ideas are ultimately put to the test.

The foregoing description is to some extent idealized, by the very nature of things. It does not deal with such major problems as the ability of administrators, particularly at the federal level, to use the system's complexity to insulate themselves and their programs from efforts at change; the problems of sheer complexity as a slowing factor; the built-in tendency of political leaders to pass the buck to other planes of government regardless of constitutional implications; or attempts to abuse the system by men in power in the name of its own principles. Nor does it do more than touch upon the system's ability to respond to changing problems though I would argue that, to date, the system has done very well in responding to them, if not always as fast as some would like.

The Negro and the Federal System

This is not to imply that there are no specific constraints upon Negroes within the American system. As a democratic system, American federalism rather closely mirrors the demands articulated by those who share power within it. So long as the Negroes have been excluded from a proper sharing of power, not only have their demands gone unmet but their very existence has been subject to the desires of those power-holders who sought to exclude them in the first place. Thus federalism, *per se*, has not worked against Negro participation. Southern whites, Northern bigots, working class locals, industrialist and agricultural exploiters of cheap, docile labor, and the general insensitivity of the mass of white Americans, not the federal system, have worked against Negro interests. Naturally, these whites have used the political system, which they controlled, to support their stands—whether in the extreme form of forcing racial segregation or in more "moderate" ways of simply allowing the social system to follow its usual course.

The ultimate neutrality of federalism, as such, is nowhere better illustrated than in the increasing ability of Negroes to make use of its mechanisms to gain a share of the available political power and turn it against the social system. This is really what has been happening during the past twenty years, first with the courts, then with the city councils of the more progressive cities, then with the legislatures and governors of the more progressive states, then back to the federal executive branch, to Congress, and finally with the various organs of state and local government again. Effective Negro political power, once exercised, has become a potent force because Negro demands are attuned to authentically American values that can no longer be honestly resisted by countervailing values. As Morton Grodzins has said, the true minority in America today is the segregationist minority which stands in opposition to "an idea whose time has come."

Federalism may have slowed down the pace of change somewhat, preventing the gap between political and social reality from growing too wide at any given moment. In the long run, it may also assure that the more militant Negroes will not get everything they demand but will have to make some compromises as well, for better or for worse. At the same time, federalism has enabled us to use political mechanisms to radically change the social system without shattering either. The opposition to Negro advancement along the road of equality remains strong, yet the social system has been forced to make meaningful changes. Even the compromises that will have to be made can be useful to the Negroes' cause if, for example, they should lead to a greater emphasis on self-help within the ghettos. The trick is to become involved in the decision-making process at every reasonable point in the federal system, including its crucial state and local planes. The evidence points to significant movement in that direction even now.

The New Concern with Federalism

The revival of concern for the values of noncentralized government and maximum possible local control, after a generation in which public debate was dominated by the arguments of those who deprecated federalism in favor of a

Washington-centered pluralism, should make it apparent that the need for a federalist approach to problems of human government and welfare continues undiminished. Since the 1930s—the heyday of the idea of centralized pluralism—it has become apparent to advocates of positive government as well as to old-line conservatives that power concentrated is power uncontrolled even when it is concentrated in the hands of men of good will; that institutions and programs, once created, develop a life of their own regardless of their validity under new conditions; and that bureaucracy has its own interests and problems and pursues its own goals, even when it is manned by people with the best of intentions; and taken together, the consequences of all three of the above limit the possibilities of democratic decision-making unless powers, institutions, and bureaucracies are constitutionally divided and then controlled through a system that guarantees the entire citizenry a crack at them from many angles and vantage points.

It is significant that the revived concern for what are essentially federal principles and processes represents a shifting of concern from *what* is to be done to cope with America's social problems, to *how* it is to be done. Since the Great Depression (and, among reformers, even before) the great question in the human welfare field has been the question of *what* with the *how* incidental—a matter of accommodating existing interests. Those who raised the latter question were automatically labeled conservatives or even reactionaries who placed attachment to a system ahead of a concern for human beings. Today it has become apparent that the question of *how* is not so easily dismissed, that it may be as important as *what* if the problems under attack are to be dealt with meaningfully.

Whether the *how* being advocated follows the path of "creative federalism" or that of "neighborhood self-government," its advocates reflect the new thinking about intergovernmental relations that has become dominant in the past few years. Advocacy of the diffusion of power and maximum local control is no longer predicated in the theory of dual federalism, the separation of state-local and federal functions with the concomitant minimization of the federal role. On the contrary, it assumes extensive intergovernmental cooperation with important responsibilities located on all planes and the federal government playing a significant role in one way or another. While cooperative federalism of the latter kind has existed in significant proportions since the establishment of the Republic it has only been "discovered" in the last generation.[9] Because of the experiences and studies of the past thirty years, today's efforts consciously begin with a recognition of the intergovernmental partnership. In fact, they may well be directed toward the task of turning a "merely" intergovernmental partnership into a truly federal one.

The preceding summary of the discussion of diffusing power and increasing local control has been reworded in the terminology of federalism. While this terminology is not always used by the advocates of creative federalism and is rarely found among the advocates of neighborhood self-government, it is implicit in their approach to the problems at hand. In fact, the future refinement of either approach rests, to no little extent, on the refinement of their understanding of the federal principles and processes which can make it possible.

It is precisely at this point that the two approaches begin to diverge. Creative federalism, after all, is something of a catch phrase designed to supply a rationale for a radical expansion of the existing intergovernmental partnership coupled with some adjustments in sharing arangements. It is based on two fundamental premises: (1) *governmental activities must be shared by all levels of government to be effective and to be responsive to public needs* and (2) *it is possible for all governments simultaneously to grow in power.*[10] The first, in effect, recognizes that the various governments in the United States are more likely to share common interests, which encourage or demand intergovernmental cooperation for their satisfaction or achivement, than they are to be in conflict. The second holds that governmental power is not a limited quantity, a pie that must be redivided with every new program giving one government a greater share at the expense of the others, but itself expands so that all governments may gain power simultaneously. For the purposes of those espousing the "creative federalism" approach, the latter premise is particularly important since it gives the federal government a well-nigh blank check for future expansion so long as it does not formally attempt to preempt functions or otherwise seek to eliminate the state and local role.

Beyond these fundamental premises, "creative federalism" covers a multitude of efforts, activities, and approaches ranging from President Johnson's proposals to increase the share of federal aid to the states and localities by tens of billions of dollars to Senator Muskie's efforts to improve the administration and coordination of grant programs; from the governors' interest in channeling more federal aid through the states' elected leadership to the big city mayors' desire to forge a more direct federal-city relationship.[11] Among its concrete manifestations in the past few years are included:

1. Doubling the number of major federal grant programs, up from well under 100 in 1960, to 162 in 1966.
2. Expansion of the dollar amount of federal transfers of payments to the states and localities and the percentage of federal funds in state and local expenditures from 7 billion dollars and 10 percent in 1960 to 13 billion dollars and 13 percent in 1966.
3. Addition of major new federal responsibilities[12] in such fields as antipoverty, civil rights, conservation, consumer protection, education, hospital insurance, automobile and highway safety, food and drug inspection, urban rehabilitation, and environmental pollution control; most of which have led to substantial or increased state and local involvement as well.
4. Experimentation with new forms of federal-state collaboration such as the Appalachian Regional Commission, the Delaware River Basin Commission and their counterparts in other regions or river basins which are designed to give the states a role in the initial policy-making process equal to that of Washington.
5. An increase in direct federal-local relations, particularly in the fields of urban social and physical redevelopment coupled with at least a formal effort to stimulate greater state participation in these activities.
6. Efforts to simplify intergovernmental administrative relations

through improving coordination, streamlining organization, and opening better channels of communication between the three planes of government.

7. Efforts to involve general governmental leaders at the state level —governors and legislators—in cooperative activities through greater interlevel consultation and the expansion of state planning functions as means of general governmental control.

8. Modification of some federal grant programs in the direction of block grants to encourage the flexible use of federal aid in the states under comprehensive state plans.

9. Direct federal intervention into local problems on a number of fronts, particularly in connection with civil rights and antipoverty programs.

10. Increased federal-private partnership arrangements that pay scant attention to the state and local governments, particularly in the case of programs like the Job Corps sponsored by the Office of Economic Opportunity.

11. Some attempts to extend federal powers unilaterally in programs traditionally shared, particularly in those fields under the jurisdiction of the Department of Labor.[13]

If creative federalism has little in the way of coherent theory but much in the form of concrete action to delineate its meaning, the neighborhood–self-government approach is in just the opposite condition. The idea of neighborhood self-government has its roots in the very old tradition of the small republic. Indeed, some proponents of neighborhood self-government quote the Antifederalists and Thomas Jefferson as authoritative American expressions of the small-republic tradition. The contemporary revival of the neighborhood–self-government idea is rooted in the growing concern with the problems of the big city ghettos and in the feeling that the ghetto dwellers are cut out of the normal processes of the American system of government because they have no place at the bargaining table. It is reinforced by the emergence of communities of middle class social "dropouts" such as the hippies whose advocacy of a social revolution within "the system" through the creation of new communities has its attractions for all who seek radical improvements in the social order. Occasionally it is espoused as a tactic by those who seek total revolution in American society. While the advocates of creative federalism are primarily concerned with achieving greater efficiency in government, the advocates of neighborhood self-government are primarily concerned with achieving greater community. Both ideas have their place in American thought and in relation to one another.

The problems of race relations, poverty, and alienation force us to confront our political system "in the raw" and assess its progress. They also offer Americans an opportunity to consider the possibilities of a truly creative federalism beyond the limits of ghettos, urban or rural. For the truth is that less than one fifth of all Americans are directly faced with the problem of poverty while less than 10 percent are faced with the problems of racial discrimination and poverty together. Yet all Americans are faced with the larger problems to which "creative federalism" and "neighborhood self-government" speak: the problems of the proper role and functioning of government, democratic decision-making, and community identity, among others; hence the necessity of dealing with the ghettos is also an opportunity to reopen questions seemingly closed by recently established orthodoxies and undertake tasks appropriate to meeting those questions.

Developing a Truly Creative Federalism

At this moment we should take advantage of an enforced slowdown in "new starts" to consider those questions and plot future courses of action consistent with the principles of federalism, especially since the effects of the Vietnam war and the civil rights revolution are likely to have consequences far beyond the limitation or fulfillment of the specific schemes of creative federalism.

Following the pattern of reform established over generations since the founding of the Republic, the development of nationwide pressures for action to meet current problems culminated in a short period of intense action in Washington. That action established a new base from which to proceed with social improvement while at the same time exhausting public demands for substantial innovation on a national basis. If the pattern continues as it has in the past (and there is every sign that it will), the thrust for social improvement has now passed to those charged with implementing the new programs and giving them firmer shape—the states and localities on one side and the federal bureaucracy on the other.[14] The very nature of the social innovations enacted by the "Great Society" Congresses makes this well-nigh inevitable. Mostly grant-in-aid programs involving federal stimulation of state and local activity, their complexity gave the federal bureaus an important role in determining just how the states and localities are to be assisted and, in some cases, which ones will obtain aid.

The social welfare field is one in which some important questions have been raised and others need to be. When the American governments moved into the social welfare field on a massive scale a generation ago, important new ideas of federal action, national standard-setting, the relationship between large monetary expenditures and successful public welfare programs, and the need for a new social work profession captured the imagination of policy-makers and their advisers. Together these ideas led to the development of a bundle of programs which serve as the basis for the nation's social welfare system and which have done much to reorient American thinking about the necessity and legitimacy of government action in the social welfare field. However, as is usually the case in such matters, today these same ideas have crystallized into an orthodoxy which leads to uncritical attempts to apply them in every current situation.[15] The proponents of creative federalism have initiated some efforts to modify that orthodoxy while the proposals for neighborhood self-government at least implicitly challenge its very foundations. The lack of apparent progress in dealing with the problems of the ghettos has stimulated the kind of criticism of current programs by various left-of-center critics that was previously heard only from the right. Congress has tried to meet some of those criticisms through the expansion of programs aimed at rehabilitation of welfare recipients and their restoration to the ranks of society's productive members. Increased congressional interest in integrated broad-gauged public health services is another reflection of the new trend, as is much of the antipoverty legislation. President Johnson, in turn, appointed a commission to study the entire welfare system with a view to proposing changes. It is in the meshing of the two approaches that the future of social welfare action in the United States may well lie.

To date, the reform efforts have not seriously departed from earlier precedents though they may prove to be the beginnings of a movement in the direction of fundamental change. What the substantive nature of these changes will be is a matter for discussion elsewhere. Here we must confine ourselves to their systemic aspects.

We have noted the recent shift of emphasis away from Washington or from new legislation, the rising tide of concern regarding the validity of established approaches, and the opportunities and constraints of the American political system. What, then, are the tasks confronting those who wish to develop a truly creative federalism by dealing with the problem of *how*? Let us start with three: 1) there is a need to revive consideration of the first principles of federalism as the basis for the effort; 2) there is a need for redefining governmental roles in light of those principles to promote better noncentralization; and 3) there is a need for rescaling governments where necessary to assume their roles and implement those principles.

For too long the demand for considering the first principles of federalism has been left to those who would try to repeal the twentieth century (and who do a bad job with federal principles in the process). The reasons for this are not difficult to understand. Especially since the 1930s, liberals have denigrated those principles because of their desire to break the encrustations of orthodoxy which had come to surround them, preventing the kind of action then needed to come to grips with the twentieth century. Those opposed to them reacted in kind.

The success of the New Deal elevated American pragmatism from a useful technique into the nation's central principle and, in the process, substantive concern with federalism was shunted aside, to be used only when pragmatically convenient. As a means of shaking off the shackles of earlier constitutional interpretations, this approach was eminently successful and, so long as men who had been raised in the earlier pattern of constitutionalism led both the New Deal revolt and the conservative opposition to it, the spirit of referring to first principles remained, regardless of the extent to which they were bent for pragmatic ends.

Thirty years later, pragmatism has become the new orthodoxy and a generation has arisen which was not formed with the old Constitutional habits. As a result, we have the paradox of Negroes and students calling for the most traditional of American rights, that of community self-government, and believing themselves to be revolutionaries unalterably opposed to the American system only to be opposed in their quest by spokesmen for the system who view their request simply as an assault by "outs" on the established order.

To confuse matters further, the supposed friends of "creative federalism" explicitly or implicitly believe that large-scale organizations ordered hierarchically represent the only way to solve today's problems. Unconsciously committed to thinking of hierarchical patterns—of "levels" of government, of centrally established uniformities of programs and procedure, and of local governments as glorified field offices of Washington designed to implement explicit national policies to the letter—they view constitutional and radical demands for real noncentralization as obsolete. They seem to be saying, over and again, that such demands must, perforce, lead to "chaos," "overlapping," and "inefficiency," basing their judgment on present standards of business efficiency, first and foremost.[16]

Consideration of the principles of federalism should lead to a recognition of several logical consequents, some of which are noted here: (1) The continued diffusion of power in the face of relentless pressures toward its concentration, present in every political system, is contingent upon constitutionally fixed—even if flexible—institutional arrangements for its equitable distribution, as well as for procedural safeguards. (2) Territorial divisions are indeed the best possible means for attaining the equitable expression of the country's variegated interests. (3) A decent society involves the maintenance of viable communities. (4) True liberty means the right of polities and individuals to make mistakes or refuse to live up to the highest standards in every case. Finally (5), a little chaos is a necessary concomitant of meaningful freedom.

Recognition of the foregoing, in turn, leads to less emphasis on strengthening the hierarchical elements in the American system with the kind of centralized planning that accompanies such elements, and more on strengthening the mosaic of governments with the kind of state and community-oriented planning (seen in part in the "advocacy planning" presently being promoted among certain reformers) that serves the mosaic as such. Recognition of the ideas listed above should lead to a realization that, just because a problem exists nationwide, it does not need to be solved nationally and perhaps cannot be solved except locally. Such reasoning would restore the idea that ours is a nation of states, not simply by accident but for good democratic reasons. Despite the great increase in hierarchical thinking stimulated by both the business and older reformist elements and the concomitant increase in hierarchical organization in American government, the force of the traditional political system has continued to function to modify the impact of such tendencies. The noncentralized party system and its chief governmental arm, the Congress of the United States, keeps even the existing hierarchies open to public influence at many levels by allowing and encouraging political intervention on behalf of constituents and constituent interests. By doing so, it renders them more useful as well as more responsible. However, the continued pressure on the traditional system for its ostensible inefficiencies—those aspects which keep it open—is having its effect.

Reflection on the principles of federalism should lead to efforts to strengthen civil communities at the expense of the new irresponsible social (and intellectual) individualism just as the ideas of the 1930s led to the strengthening of civil society at the expense of irresponsible economic individualism. The problem of community has always taken on unique characteristics in the United States where traditional communities have never been common but it is only in our own time that the establishment and maintenance of desired community

norms by local consensus has come under continued assault
in the name of individual liberties. This, in itself, has func-
tioned to put several of the most promising intraghetto movements beyond the pale of acceptability even among American
political leaders of good will, because they advocate a measure
of self-segregation. Over the next few years, we may have
to seriously re-evaluate the wisdom of our present policy
that prevents communities from establishing certain restrictive
regulations in order to preserve or create their own patterns
of living. Whether in regard to the location of chain stores,
the provision of special educational services, or the prohibi-
tion of pornographic literature, we may come to recognize
the validity of the kind of federalism of communities which
traditionally formed the basis of American society.

Finally, this reasoning based on the principles of federalism
should lead to the restoration of serious dialogue about the
meaning of the Constitution in matters other than those
involving individual liberties. Since the shift in United States
Supreme Court interpretation of the commerce clause and
the Fourteenth Amendment in 1937, the Court has tended to
downgrade "boundary" questions and abdicate decisions involving the distribution of powers among the planes of governments to the political bodies. While this approach had
many virtues, it also has led to a progressive denigration of
constitutional considerations, as such, in response to immediate
political pressures. Without a more or less system-oriented
body to speak for the Constitution, the temptation to follow
the lines of least political resistance becomes overwhelming,
whether they lead to actions good in the long run or not.

The restoration of this sense of the Constitution is likely
to upset many myths, both liberal and conservative; to require
reconsideration of many theories and some practices; and
even to prevent some kinds of actions.[17] At the same time, it
will open up new opportunities for the development of the
kind of community-oriented government that an increasing
number of reformers are coming to perceive as the key to
meeting the problems of the ghettos—and our urban civilization generally—the only kind of government that can sustain
the "whole man" approach to human rehabilitation.

Toward a Federalism of Communities

With the recourse to first principles, there will also be a need to redefine governmental roles, rescale governmental institutions, and redirect public actions, emphasizing the crucial place of communities and states in the American scheme of things. In doing that it will be possible to integrate the concerns of creative federalism which can provide the organizational wherewithal for problem-solving, with the drive for neighborhood self-government which may increasingly provide the humanistic base. There are both pragmatic and profound reasons for pursuing this course. In the first place, the states and localities remain important bases of political power, policy-making, and administration within the political system which can be ignored only at some peril. Second, the states and localities can and do serve as important focal points for decision-making and innovation in the system.

Beyond that, however, the great tendency of the 1960s, particularly among those who will take over the reins of public and civic activity in the future, has been toward widened participation in public affairs, toward making governmental activity the personal activity of citizens. No doubt this trend is set by a minority but it is a large and significant one. It is possible that the emphasis on participation is a passing one. My reading of the evidence, however, leads me to believe that it is not; that there is an honest search for what Henry Hart has called "a community-defining federalism" to overcome the problems of bigness inherent in a nation of over 200 million people which has, to date, used technology to promote a mass society, often at the expense of community.[18]

This search is likely to be intensified as part of the expanding question of *how*. The end of its quest is likely to be an effort to restore community, not in some romantic sense of *Gemeinschaft* but at the very least in the sense of "civil community"—a community organized and defined essentially for civic and political reasons, involving continuation and expansion of real decision-making powers within a local community scaled down to manageable size. This is the meaning of neighborhood self-government, as I understand it. Such a meaning extends notions of community participation that grew out of the civil rights struggle and the war on poverty, but it goes beyond both the spontaneous participation that marked the former and the institutionalized consultation that was supposed to mark the latter, toward a situation in which the participants can function through community institutions vested with appropriate local responsibility—functioning as meaningful parts of the sharing system, not in isolation from it.

Part of the problem of the ghettos today is the fuller integration of their residents into the American political system. This process is certainly retarded by submerging the ghetto residents in the nation's largest cities where the connections between the average citizen and the world of political decision-making are necessarily weakest. As long as the major drive for Negro rights was primarily for enforcing legal demands at the highest level, the ability of Negroes to govern themselves locally was less important than their ability to stir white consciences in the nation as a whole. Because of its very successes, that struggle has now turned to less dramatic tasks, to the maintenance of a proper voice in the governmental game day in and day out. That is a task rendered more difficult for Negroes when they must first carve a niche for themselves in their own localities in the face of the political and administrative complexities of big city government.

The fact is that the proponents of neighborhood self-government, while directing their attention toward the problems of the biggest cities and their ghettos, have been anticipated in most of their demands for a community-level seat in the great game of government by the great majority of Americans in their movement to the suburbs. The antisuburban bias that all too often afflicts the most vocal commentators on the contemporary scene has obscured this basic fact: the suburban migration with the suburbs' concomitant jealous regard for their respective integrities has reflected a search, however imperfect, for communities better scaled as local governments than the big cities. The phenomenon of suburbanization, which involves settlement of rural and small town migrants in suburbs as well as the out-migration of city populations, can and should be viewed as a vote for the reduction of the scale of local government to the manageable proportions familiar to a society with rural and small town roots and biases. In many cases the suburbs have provided just such benefits of scale as intended and have enabled their residents to secure a degree of control over their immediate environment—over such important matters as education, law enforcement, and aesthetic controls—plus a real chance to function as citizens. Today the overwhelming majority of all Americans live in suburban, nonmetropolitan, or rural cities or communities of potentially local scale that could become meaningful participatory communities of one sort or another, and they do not intend to give up that chance.[19]

It is the urban poor (and the great majority of urban Negroes, poor or not), the students, and the other vocal critics of "the system" who are located in cities the very size of which prevents them from being meaningful *local* governments. These groups do, indeed, have reason to demand reform. In fact, by doing so they show themselves to be as highly committed to American values as their neighbors who have chosen the suburbs, and equally desirous of attaining communities which reflect *their* life-style preferences. As they are presently structured, however, the big cities which house these groups cannot satisfy this need. As long as big cities are considered local governments, as in any suburb or small city, they will not be able to do so.

Unfortunately, many of the same people who seek meaningful local governments in the name of community seek to eliminate (either *de jure* or *de facto*) existing local governments in the name of efficiency. The high concern for metropolitan government in some form is one aspect of the Johnson administration's creative federalism. The major new urban programs enacted by Congress generally require some steps in the direction of metropolitan decision-making. The Department of Housing and Urban Development is diligently engaged in enforcing those requirements. While metropolitan coordination is of undoubted value in many cases, the larger drive for metropolitan decision-making, whether in the form of complete consolidation or through the transfer of crucial local functions to a metropolitan-wide authority, reflects the tendency to seek efficiency-oriented solutions in place of communitarian ones. Though such a course is often advanced in the name of humanistic values, the ghettos are likely to suffer most from it, because it further dilutes their political power and makes their residents further dependent upon the good will of others.

Regardless of the original merit (or lack of it) in the metropolitan-government argument, the growth of megalopolis with its long chains of contiguous yet separate communities, criss-crossed with patterns of mobility and commerce, makes metropolitan area-centered solutions obsolete. At the same time, the emergence of so many interconnected but independent communities each of relatively equal importance, makes possible the development of new ways to mobilize regional resources in support of greater local self-government on the community level.

Herein lies one of the problems that must be overcome in order to have a truly creative federalism. The fostering of truly local government must be given high priority, whether by improving suburban governments, strengthening rural communities, or even breaking up the big cities. That is one of the larger meanings of neighborhood self-government and, indeed, of creative federalism. Federalism itself offers the best possibility for accomplishing this. The arguments for small-scale community are counterbalanced to no little degree by arguments for the efficiencies of large-scale governmental activity in certain fields. The American federal system offers a way to have both, through the very principles and processes of noncentralization and partnership discussed above. Metropolitan government and big cities do not obviate the need for federal and state assistance, but that assistance can eliminate the need for oversized local governmental structures while still providing appropriate levels of service. Now that we understand it better, it is possible to build upon the American partnership, not to try the impossible task of separating functions by government but by capitalizing on the necessity for sharing to properly allocate roles among participating governments.

Local governments should be so scaled that they can effectively serve and speak for local publics, not consolidated in a vain effort to function as central governments. Those publics who do not have local governments of sufficiently intimate scale should be encouraged to get them. To the best of my knowledge, in all of our discussions about the urban ghetto (including discussions about the movement of jobs away from city-dwellers) nobody has suggested the development of new towns for ghetto dwellers, outside the big cities, with independent local governments of their own—in other words, capitalizing on the possibilities inherent in the federal system to extend its advantages.

Old and New Roles for the States

In many respects, the efficiencies of scale can be best met by the states or state-related regional authorities, which can aggregate resources and talents without cutting both off from the local community, while moderating interlocal jealousies and conflicts. The role of the state, already greater than most people realize, needs to be enhanced in ways that are just beginning to become apparent.[20] Already definers, coordinators and administrators, the states must additionally be encouraged to develop what might be called "backstopping" skills within a locally oriented system: the ability to diagnose local programs, to expose local goals, implicit as well as articulated, for public consideration and scrutiny within the civil community; and ultimately, to aid in the evaluation of both programs and goals in light of local and larger interests. Such state governments will be able to aid and guide their small governmental subdivisions in many ways without imposing new hierarchical structures upon them.

There are already many signs that the states, particularly the more progressive ones, are moving in that direction, partly as a result of federal actions in this decade and to a significant extent of their own accord even in the face of adverse federal and big-city pressures. The new approach to federal aid for public health which features block grants to the states based on comprehensive state-developed plans is illustrative of this trend. Long before the elimination of categorical grants by Congress, state departments of health were feeling their way toward a planning-stimulating-coordinating role. Their achievements, even within the limits imposed upon them by categorical assistance, were responsible for that rare success, federal acquiescence to a formal broadening of their policy-making role. They are now in a position to develop their "backstopping" role as well. Congress has recognized the possibilities for making similar efforts in other fields—education, manpower resources, even the war on poverty—sometimes with success and sometimes finding its legislative enactments frustrated by federal administrators in certain agencies responsible for implementation. These administrators, supported by their clientele groups still operating according to the orthodoxies evolved a generation ago, do all in their power to prevent the states from assuming new policy-making powers.[21]

Colleagues of mine who have served with state governments have told me of their frustrations but they have also told me—and I have observed them myself—of the opportunities they have had in the states to really influence the course of events as individuals. This leads me to think that we have neglected the possibilities inherent in the states as manageable civil societies. Too large (with a few exceptions) to be communities in the sense under consideration here, they are often of more suitable size to be meaningful and manageable republics than the United States as a whole, with its population now in excess of 200 million. As such, they offer opportunities for truly significant public participation whose limits are still unknown and whose possibilities are great indeed. The expansion and exploitation of those possibilities must necessarily be a major task for creative federalism. Some states—California, Texas, Minnesota, North Carolina, to name only a few—are already devoting governmental resources to moving along that road. We all can study their example and learn from it. Except in a few cases related to very specific issues, however, appropriate public responses have yet to develop.

The new role of the state as the primary planner, "backstopper," and source for democratic participation, then, is just beginning to emerge. Contemporary orthodoxies mitigate against its development even when the consequences of neglecting aspects of that role are apparent. Recently, workers in the vineyards of social welfare have discovered that, contrary to the orthodox view, the states can be more progressive than Congress. The fight to repeal or modify the crippling public welfare amendments enacted by the last Congress is being led, to a substantial degree, by the governors as well as the state welfare directors while Medicaid is being developed into a substantial program in spite of federal efforts to soft-pedal it, as a result of state efforts.

On another level, there have been many recent efforts to bypass the states through federal project grants to localities, ostensibly on the grounds that the states have no role to play in matters of strictly local interest. In fact, this has led to great bottlenecks in the decision-making process by forcing thousands of decisions upon single agencies in Washington, far removed from the scene of operations, rather than distributing responsibility for those decisions among fifty states (plus the territories), all closer to the local scene. Most of these project grants are designed to stimulate innovation at the local level, with a desired goal being addition to the pool of new ideas available for other communities. In fact, direct federal allocation of project grants generally restricts innovation by forcing localities into a mold that is easier to handle administratively and, at the same time, limits the exchanges of information about successful innovations to very formal reporting necessitated by the factor of scale.[22] Federal funds that could have been used to foster state competency as well as local activity thus achieve less than they potentially could.

Arguments for strengthening localities as civil communities and states as civil societies are not arguments for reducing federal activity, *per se*. Federal-generated funds, ideas, and techniques will play a major role in the nation's quest for social improvement in the foreseeable future as they have in the past. Indeed, the availability of the right kind of federal assistance is vital to the development of a true community-defining federalism. However, these arguments should raise some questions about possibly redirecting the federal role. If creative federalism with its emphasis on sharing is not to become simply an excuse for centralization of power in Washington or, more likely, concentration of power in the hands of experts and specialists who thrive when they are insulated from the publics they serve, it must lead to the use of federal resources to foster broad participation as well as to stimulate ever higher levels of achievement. This probably means that the federal role should be increasingly redirected away from narrowly prescriptive or supportive programs and toward broad actions that will stimulate states and localities to raise their sights and toward serious steps to provide the infrastructure for states and community development.

More concretely, this would mean the shifting of the quest for over-all planning away from the national plane to the states and communities and the maintenance of established patterns of national smorgasbord (improved in structure and design) that give the latter a chance to choose from a multiplicity of programs (even contradictory ones) according to their own perceived needs. The federal role would continue to be one of stimulating certain kinds of state and local activity and harmonizing state and local actions where absolutely necessary. It would also mean the use of federal regulatory powers—ranging from antitrust action to consumer protection, from the maintenance of civil rights to the regulation of freight rates—to protect individuals so that they can participate and communities so that their participation can be satisfying and meaningful. The latter set of tasks has already become important in something of a pre-emptive way, with the federal government often pitted against state and local interests. They can—and should—become even more important in the future but in more supportive ways.

Given the continued American involvement overseas that is likely to persist even after the conclusion of the Vietnam war, there is little likelihood that those representatives of the people charged with policy-making responsibilities on the federal plane will be able to devote sufficient attention to domestic concerns. Nor should they be required to, because under the Constitution their first responsibility is to foreign relations and national defense. Others can deal with the domestic side of government; nobody can replace the national government's responsibility in the realm of external affairs. Hence we must expect the continued subordination of domestic concerns at the federal level, expressed either through financial limitations or delegation of greater policy-making power to administrators, and must be prepared to look elsewhere for policy-makers with an undivided concern for domestic matters.

The searching out and development of these alternate centers of policy-making is one of the tasks of those concerned with social welfare in the years just ahead. It is part of the over-all task of synthesizing the thrust of creative federalism with the drive for neighborhood self-government into a better *how* that could possibly get to the real roots of the problems symbolized by the situation in the ghettos. The search for the *how* should involve us in redirecting the new social services of health and rehabilitation, restructuring the war on poverty, and perhaps in revising the welfare system itself, using all to develop communities that may provide sufficient support for individuals in their efforts to fit into the social order in a meaningful way.

Social welfare activists may well find themselves fighting for the creation of viable civil communities, after the pattern of their predecessors of two generations ago but with the problems of scale uppermost in their minds. They may well find themselves fighting for the recognition of community diversities the way they have struggled for the recognition of individual diversities in the past. They should also find themselves working to develop a concern for their states that is not merely program-related but which sees in those civil societies the basis for the public life of the commonwealth. They are likely to find themselves fighting the extension, as if by reflex, of entrenched patterns of doing things, including efforts to intensify the expert-oriented, pre-emptive, hier-archical approach to problem-solving that has emerged as the keystone of the present orthodoxy. And they will have to fight that approach within themselves as well as in society at large.

Federalism is particularly relevant in this context because of the very conditions which are causing many thoughtful people to reconsider the actions of the past generation. At a time when the social compact binding American civil society is being renegotiated—particularly in the ghettos and among the young—federalism, which, as the very word indicates, is concerned with the covenants that establish civil society and make its governance both possible and worthwhile, becomes a matter of pragmatic as well as polemical concern. It seems that in the very pattern of things, once every hundred years Americans are called upon to renegotiate that compact. It is precisely at such times that otherwise ignored questions of *how*—the basic question of federalism—become central to the improvement of American life.

NOTES

1. See, for example, Lyndon B. Johnson, *Message from the President of the United States Transmitting Recommendations to Improve the Quality of Government,* March 20, 1967, available as U.S. House of Representatives, 9th Congress, 1st Sess., House Document No. 90; and John Gardner, *Creative Federalism* (Washington, D.C.: U.S. Department of Health, Education and Welfare, 1967).

2. See, for example, Milton Kotler, "Two Essays on the Neighborhood Corporation," in *Urban America: Goals and Problems,* materials compiled for the Subcommittee on Urban Affairs of the Joint Economic Committee, Congress of the United States, August 1967.

3. For a fuller definition and delineation of federalism as a form of political organization, see "Federalism," in the *International Encyclopedia of the Social Sciences* (New York: Macmillan, 1968).

4. The various sources of federalism are discussed in Andrew McLaughlin, *Foundations of American Constitutionalism* (New York: Fawcett, 1961).

5. J. A. G. Griffith, *Central Departments and Local Authorities* (Toronto: University of Toronto Press, 1966).

6. See, especially, Gilbert Y. Steiner *Social Insecurity: The Politics of Welfare* (Chicago: Rand McNally, 1966); and Daniel P. Moynihan, "The Crises in Welfare," *The Public Interest* 10 (Winter 1968).

7. Steiner, in *Social Insecurity,* corroborates this from a negative point of view.

8. See Morton Grodzins, *The American System*, edited by Daniel J. Elazar (Chicago: Rand McNally, 1966), Part III.

9. Daniel J. Elazar, *The American Partnership* (Chicago: University of Chicago Press, 1962).

10. For a full discussion of these premises and their role in "Great Society" thinking, see Ways, "Creative Federalism in the Great Society," *Fortune*, January 1966.

11. An overall summary can be found in "Steps Initiated to Implement 'Creative Federalism,'" *CQ Fact Sheet*, March 24, 1967.

12. For the most complete listing of federal aid programs, see Office of Economic Opportunity, *Catalog of Federal Assistance Programs* (Washington, D.C., 1967).

13. See *CQ Fact Sheet on Federal Aid*, October 6, 1967.

14. This process is described in greater detail in Daniel J. Elazar, *Toward a Generational Theory of American Politics* (Philadelphia: Center for the Study of Federalism, 1968).

15. Moynihan, "The Crises in Welfare," indicates some ways in which this is so and how it became so.

16. For an example of this kind of hierarchical "organization" thinking, presented with the best of intentions on behalf of the maintenance of federalism, see Committee for Economic Development, *Modernizing Local Government* (New York: 1967).

17. See Martin Diamond, "Liberals, Conservatives and the Constitution," in *The Public Interest*, 1 (Fall, 1965).

18. Henry C. Hart, "The Dawn of a Community-Defining Federalism," in *The Annals of the American Academy of Political and Social Science*, 359 (May, 1965).

19. For a fuller discussion of this phenomenon see Robert Goldwin, ed., *A Nation of Cities* (Chicago: Rand McNally, 1968), particularly the articles by Wilson, Kristol, and Elazar.

20. Terry Sanford discusses these points in *Storm Over the States* (New York: McGraw-Hill, 1967).

21. See *ibid.*

22. See *Creative Federalism*, Hearings Before the Subcommittee on Intergovernmental Relations of the Committee on Government Operations, U.S. Senate, Parts 1, 2-A, and 2-B, 1966 and 1967.

8 | MELVIN B. MOGULOF

Creative Federalism, not Abdication

It is good to be reminded by Daniel Elazar that yesterday's conservative can sound like today's liberal. Many of us who remember when the argument for state's rights was a mask for racism, will now have to relearn that state's rights can mean "participatory democracy." But this is not to imply that the state is Dr. Elazar's key governmental unit in his search for that system which best provides for a sense of community and the opportunity to influence the way we shall be governed. Creative federalism is described to us as a "noncentralization with power so distributed that the rank order of the several governments is not fixed." But by sheer accumulation of words and ideas, the discourse makes clear that there is a rank order in Dr. Elazar's mind of a governmental unit which can best insure a sense of participation—that unit being the local municipality. And in the name of a certain kind of efficiency which is decried in the move toward regionalization of local governments, it is proposed to break large cities into smaller cities. Local governments should be so scaled as to "effectively serve and speak for local publics."

In its generality, so far, so good. One might quibble and argue that the most significant publics many people participate in are those which do not cross (or have little relevance to)

This chapter is a response to the preceding chapter by Daniel J. Elazar.

political jurisdictions (e.g., professional associations, work groups, unions, political parties, minority protective associations). The very fact of belonging to publics whose memberships cross political boundaries may be true primarily for the cosmopolitans and middle class among us. If the poor are denied access to boundary-crossing publics by virtue of their poverty, then we at least ought to provide a local community game for them to play. In fact the provision of this game might even cover our failure to provide them with much else. Although, of course, the argument undoubtedly is that entrance into a manageable community game will be instrumental toward the procuring of bread, the empirical evidence for this assumption is slim.

It is at the point that Dr. Elazar begins to speak of scaling local governments to local publics that he puts on display the logical imperative of his form of creative federalism. He writes "to the best of my knowledge, in all of our discussions about the urban ghetto . . . nobody has suggested the development of new towns for ghetto dwellers." So there you have it—apartheid American style in the name of creative federalism. I think Dr. Elazar claims too much credit when he implies that he may be the first to suggest this idea. At the very least, the Germans and the South Africans have had pertinent experience with ghettoized new towns. Now, ten years ago the National Conference on Social Welfare might have hooted a speaker off the platform for this suggestion; seven years ago the conference might have (it didn't, to its discredit, did it?) invited Malcolm X to say these things, if it had known he was saying them. This year an academic with impressive credentials gives us this framework for apartheid American-style, and we must listen to him and deal with the argument. As he has reminded us, yesterday's conservative is today's liberal.

Of course, Dr. Elazar is not an isolated white academic preaching racial separatism. He is in the stream of the most sensitive, embittered, brilliant black thinkers in our country who have said to hell with integration—give us some place where we can control our destinies as black people. But as with other converts, he goes his mentors one better. He writes, "we may have to seriously re-evaluate the wisdom of our present policy that prevents communities from establishing certain restrictive regulations in order to preserve or create their own pattern of living." (If this be the new liberal rhetoric, I trust that we will recognize its antecedents in laws against miscegenation, restrictive covenants, and other flowerings of local option.) Now this may well be the way it will have to be in our country. The chance for a multiracial society may have been lost by our years of stupidity and barbarism; and writers like Richard Cloward and Frances Piven are right in describing how the Negro poor have paid for our prattlings about integration.

But if we as social workers are going to be fed the bitter fruit of separatism, let it be in its own name—not under the guise of creative federalism.

If the logic of Dr. Elazar's creative federalism takes him to the all-black municipalities that now exist in Michigan, Missouri, Maryland, and other parts of the South, his position on the public welfare system is no less interesting. He begins by pointing out that "with the exception of OASI and veterans services, all federal social welfare programs are tied to the system of territorial democracy." I assume that a hallowed part of such territorial democracy is the right to set budgets below minimum survival needs, the right to impose residence requirements, the right to assign 150 cases to a worker, the right to search for a man in the house, the right to suggest sterilization, and all of those other rights so jealously guarded by states and counties in administering welfare. These will be recognized, of course, as "restrictive regulations in order to create or preserve their own pattern of living." The latter quotation would seem to be a key notion in Dr. Elazar's concept of creative federalism and its concomitant of territorial democracy.

Indeed the variety of ways in which public welfare is administered at the local level, accords nicely with the argument that "there is a shift of concern from *what* is to be done to *how* it is to be done." Indeed, territorial democracy has provided us with a wonderful array of *how* it is to be done in public welfare. The fact is that it is wrong, dead wrong, to argue that "there is an exhausting of public demand for in-

novation on a national basis." Every social worker is, or ought
to be sick to death of the *how* of public welfare as it is administered in the model of Dr. Elazar's creative federalism.
And there is, or ought to be, no social worker who is as
exhausted as Dr. Elazar seems to be with the demand for
innovation on a national basis. Elazar to the contrary, in public
welfare we are much more concerned with *what* than with
how. We want to enhance the *what* of cash transfer, involved
in public welfare so as to secure adequate support levels for
all poor people, whether it be through negative income tax,
guaranteed annual wage, forms of family allowance, or whatever. And we will talk increasingly and fight for the federal
government as an employer of last resort, because we know
that in our society we are defined as men and women by the
work we do with our head and our hands. And to this date
the private sector of the economy has not understood that
point. Few of us are afraid of giving those below us the same
kind of access to medical care that we have begun to give to
older people on a national basis. And there isn't an informed
person, least of all Dr. Elazar, who doesn't know that these
fights will have to be won in the national arena.

But unfortunately the paper argues differently. In Dr.
Elazar's outlook for creative federalism, not only is he prepared to make legitimate the separation of people by color; he
is also prepared to transfer consideration of domestic issues
to a level of government other than the federal, since he sees
that level as too occupied with foreign affairs. This separation
of the internal and external affairs of our nation as proposed
in Dr. Elazar's discourse, seems to come at a time when the
interconnection between such affairs seems more and more
profound. (I refer to yesterday's news, today's and tomorrow's.) Frankly, Dr. Elazar might even have switched it the
other way. It would be more interesting to have a competition
of foreign policies, vis-à-vis China let us say, than the existing one to see which state can keep their poor people surviv-
ing on the lowest possible budget.

Nothing in these comments is meant to deny the concern
for increasing chances for participatory democracy. But
whether we need to do this in a fashion which denies and

corrupts the experience we have had with national standard setting is questionable. It is particularly questionable in terms of black and white and rich and poor.

It is said that President Kennedy prior to his 1960 campaign was very attracted to the Madison Avenue agency which ran the VW campaign to "think small." He used that agency, but it is doubtful whether he let himself be influenced by its old slogans. I suggest that in Dr. Elazar's great capacity to be concerned for the smallest of us, he not lose the capacity to think big. In fact on the issues of black and white, rich and poor, and war and peace, it would appear that we need thinking which goes far beyond the nation–state, rather than sanctifying difference so that nations may continue to engage freely in "restrictive regulations in order to preserve or create their own patterns of living." We may none of us survive that particular form of anarchy.

COMMENTS: DANIEL J. ELAZAR

THE emergence of ultraconservative Republicans under the age of forty in the Southern states in the early 1960's popularized the term "young fogies" as eminently descriptive of people whose stands on current public issues were determined by unswerving allegiance to an outmoded ideology developed by preceding generations but swallowed by them whole hog. The last years of this decade are witnessing the emergence of a new group of young fogies, people under forty who have swallowed the liberal ideology of the 1930s as completely as their opposite numbers have the conservative ideology of the 1890s. One hesitates to draw the obvious conclusion but the hand of liberal young fogeyism seems suspiciously present in the preceding comments.

At a time when young people (those under thirty at least) are discovering how hollow are the ties that ostensibly bind the "publics" created by "professional associations, work groups, unions, political parties, minority protective associations" (the stuff of which 1930s-style pluralism was to have been built to overcome the stuffy conservatism of territorial communities whose ties transcended occupations and generations), we are told that attempts to overcome the alienation that seems to be characteristic of modern life with its ultra-cosmopolitan orientation are, by their very nature, reactionary and—the ultimate insult—segregationist.

The argument of my paper is simple: The only way in which Afro-Americans or any Americans can truly participate in American life is through functioning membership in meaningful local political communities. This is not an argument that the local community is the be-all and end-all of public life. It is certainly not an argument for the creation of homogeneous (or segregated) communities as the norm. It simply presents a universal truth that even the liberal ideologists cannot repeal; that basic political loyalties must commence with meaningful ties to one's neighbors and one's place of residence. In a democracy, this universal truth has a corollary; responsible political life must commence with real possibilities for participation in meaningful political decision-making, something that can only come for the overwhelming majority of the citizenry in the local community. Our alienated young, white and black, are living testimony to these universal truths. We are paying a high price for ignoring them.

To have meaning, any federalism of communities would have to offer options to all Americans to choose the form of their local community within the very broad framework of the national constitution. I choose, for a number of reasons, to live in a neighborhood that happens to be racially and religiously integrated, one that shows considerable promise of becoming a successful symbiotic community uniting several different groups which share certain minimal needs that draw them together. At the same time, I would hardly have the audacity to deny the right to others—Amish, Hassidic Jews, or black separatists—to try to create homogenous communities of their own if such is their preference. It seems to me that elementary justice dictates that the federal government provide aid to such groups equivalent to that provided through FHA and various urban improvement grants for Americans in the mainstream, particularly when new towns, all black or not, may mean the difference between a lifetime in the big-city slums or a pleasant environment for raising children, between being far from where the jobs are and being close.

Territorial democracy, like any other form of political organization, has its failings and breeds its problems. I would still submit that it is preferable to any other form that has been offered us. In any case, it is a matter of fact that our political system operates that way—often making progress as well as occasionally retarding it—and any improvements we are likely to make in dealing with our problems are likely to come only if we work with our system rather than against it. As anyone familiar with my understanding of American federalism knows, this is not an "either/or" matter, a question of eliminating the role of the federal government, of "thinking small" rather than "thinking big," but of knowing what kind of role federal government, the states, and local governments should play in the common partnership. That is to say, knowing when the American penchant for "bigger and better" no longer serves and thinking small is the only right way to think at all.

CHARLES I. SCHOTTLAND

Federal Agencies, National Associations, and the Politics of Welfare

Even those who were the most uninformed and uninterested in the "politics of welfare," became interested and many became involved in the politics which surrounded the passage of the Social Security Amendments of 1967. Some hailed the Amendments as providing the largest increase in old-age benefits since the passage of the Social Security Act, while twenty national voluntary organizations declared that the bill made "second-class citizens of persons dependent on public assistance by applying discriminatory standards to their behavior or offering them lesser protections than those available to other persons."[1] While some federal officials saw the work incentives as ushering in a "new look" in public assistance, professional social workers "deplored" those provisions which would bring pressure upon AFDC mothers to leave their children and go to work.[2] National welfare organizations applauded certain features of the bill, such as the raising of child welfare authorizations, while at the same time deploring other features. Practically all national welfare associations expressed opposition to the freeze on AFDC caseloads. While many anxiously awaited the bill's approval by the President because it meant money in the pockets of millions of OASDHI beneficiaries, organized labor in a telegram from Walter Reuther, urged the President to veto the bill because of its AFDC provisions.

Most of these actions took place during November and December of 1967, which were indeed months when the "politics of welfare" was a hit theme in the social welfare arena.

Importance of the Politics of Welfare

Until recently, the "politics of welfare" has received little attention by political writers, social scientists, or students of government. Only in the last few years has it become an increasingly popular theme in academic and welfare arenas and there is still a paucity of literature or reliable studies upon which one might base valid generalizations or conclusions.[3] This is indeed surprising in view of the fact that for the past several years, hardly a day has passed without some newspaper story of sit-ins by public welfare clients; attacks by Congressmen, public officials, business leaders, politicians, and others on AFDC; "relief chiselers"; crackdowns by the federal bureaucracy on state attempts to violate federal law or regulation; abolition of the means test; the financial soundness or unsoundness of social security; baby black markets; court decisions declaring that state laws establishing state residence as an eligibility requirement for public assistance are invalid; or challenging the traditional concept of financial responsibility of relatives; or declaring unconstitutional the long-accepted state practice of setting maximum payments to a family on public assistance; debates in Congress on poverty programs, public assistance, social security, Medicare, Medicaid, etc.; and hundreds of other items which make welfare daily reading or viewing or hearing in our public communications media.

In addition to this public interest in welfare programs, welfare programs are subject to continuous scrutiny because of the huge public expenditures involved. Even defining "welfare" narrowly to include public assistance, public child welfare, social insurance, and related programs, the annual expenditures exceed 50 billion dollars. Both in terms of money and the significant role welfare programs play in the lives of millions of persons, the politics of welfare involves huge stakes.

The recent riots in the ghettos have also placed the politics of welfare in the forefront. Everyone seems to be discovering a startling fact; namely, that there are poverty-stricken racial ghettos in every major city of America. It took the riots to establish this firmly in the mind of the average citizen. As Winston Churchill has so aptly remarked, "Nothing sharpens our thinking processes as much as the knowledge that we are going to be hanged tomorrow." It was the ghetto crisis that brought welfare and related programs to the attention of people generally, and resulted in frantic action on the part of public officials, both elected and appointed, national organizations, and other action groups. To many of the newcomers in the arena of politics, it came as somewhat of a shock and surprise to learn that once the need of the ghetto was made known it did not automatically follow that the need was met, and many workers in the newer poverty programs found it difficult to comprehend the obstacles in the way of getting programs established.

One would expect that all of this public interest would lead to more study of the politics of welfare. Perhaps one reason it has not is that welfare programs (particularly public assistance) are not a matter of continuous concern and attention but of sporadic interest.

As any experienced person knows, public programs are established through the political process, and the political process has many aspects—public feeling, the values of legislators and bureaucrats, the organized pressures which can be brought to bear during the political process, the problem of fund allocations and availability of funds, and a variety of other matters which need not be elaborated here.

Any discussion of the role of federal agencies and national organizations must be based on certain underlying considerations. Large-scale organizations are a fact of American life. General Motors has an income in excess of most of the countries of the world. The Social Security Administration employs more people than the entire civil service of many member countries of the United Nations. The federal government bureaucracies in the "welfare" field spend more than the entire national government expenditures (including military expenditures) of all but five or six countries. Although not spending as much money, the national voluntary organizations in health and welfare are growing larger and more numerous.

How do these national and federal government organizations interact with each other? What are their respective roles in the "politics of welfare?"

We must begin with the realization that governing is the province of the few. In a democracy the majority of the people, or even any substantial number of the people, do not decide on specific things such as fund allocations or what the law should be. It is very rarely that basic policy issues are presented to the body politic; rather, the people elect officials who establish the basic policies and the basic procedures under which bureaucrats who administer the policies and who themselves make policy are appointed. If the electorate does not like what is being done, they can throw out the elected officials or bring pressure upon them or upon public administrative officials.

Similarly, the national voluntary organizations are governed by the few even though they may represent the thinking of the majority—which sometimes they do (and sometimes they do not).

In terms of national associations and federal agencies, therefore, the politics of welfare may be viewed on the basis of the relationships between the few who control federal agencies and the few who occupy the leadership roles in national voluntary associations. The few leaders of the bureaucracy are the initiators of most federal legislation; their support is almost required for a proposed bill to pass since little legislation is enacted by Congress which the bureaucracy opposes. Also, funds to implement legislation depend upon the fund allocation process in which the federal agencies usually play the initiating and leading role.

Some Functions of National Associations

If national associations are to be influential in the establishment and implementation of programs in the welfare field, they must relate to the leadership in federal agencies. Their ability to influence these leaders in their decision-making and fund-allocation processes may be more important in terms of services to clients or enhancement of welfare programs than many of the more customary activities of such national associations.

There are so many ways of looking at this problem that any brief analysis or approach is bound to be partial and fragmentary. Nevertheless, it may be useful to look at the national voluntary association and its relationship to federal agencies with regard to eight specific aspects.

1. The national voluntary association as promoter and reformer. The national voluntary associations of today are the inheritors of a long tradition of political action to better the life of the American people. The names of Owen Lovejoy, Florence Kelley, Julia Lathrop, Grace and Edith Abbott, Jane Addams, Lillian Wald, Frances Perkins, Paul Kellogg, John Commons, Mary Dewson, Mary Van Kleek—to name only a few—still represent a period in the first thirty years of the twentieth century unmatched in American social welfare history.[4] Florence Kelley was an example of that time. Starting with the idea that education was the way to progress, she soon found that study, recommendation, and education moved too slowly and she moved quickly into the political arena. The National Consumers' League of which she was the secretary played a major role in promoting child labor laws, safety conditions, pure food laws, women's suffrage, maternal and child health. Margaret Robins, President of the Women's Trade Union League, also joined in political action and evolved concepts which influenced later legislation—concepts such as the living wage, economic security, "rights," and health insurance. The major religious organizations joined the growing chorus of national associations engaged in social reform during the first third of this century. In 1919, a national Protestant group, the Federal Council of Churches of Christ, revised its liberal and famous social creed of 1912 and urged adequate wages, public works, social insurance, an eight-hour day, minimum wage laws, decent housing, and equality before the law for Negroes. The National Catholic Welfare Council demanded guarantees for labor to organize and bargain effectively, minimum wages, abolition of child labor. In 1920 the Central Conference of American Rabbis joined in similar demands and asked for antilynch laws and unrestricted immigration.[5]

The zeal of these early reformers was nowhere more evident than in the campaign against child labor. Here the reformers and their national associations formed an alliance with the only federal welfare bureaucracy of the time; namely, the United States Children's Bureau. Through the combined efforts of federal officials and reformers, Congress sought to establish standards of regulation for child labor. The Supreme Court promptly declared the law unconstitutional holding that it was ". . . repugnant to the Constitution. It not only transcends the authority delegated to Congress over commerce but also exerts a power as to a purely local matter to which the federal authority does not extend."[6] The social reformers immediately pressured the Congress to try another way of controlling child labor. But this second attempt likewise was declared unconstitutional.

These rebuffs by the courts and some legislative bodies did not discourage the reformers. All through the 1920s the voluntary associations continued to press for women's rights, minimum wages, and abolition of child labor.

It was growing professionalization of social work combined with the emphasis on psychological individualization that seemed to blur the reform movements in social welfare. Following the First World War, social work began to move toward an approach "with greater emphasis on adjusting the individual than on changing the society."[7] The emergence of social casework with its focus on techniques of working with individual clients, the debates between the generic and specialized casework advocates, the extension of casework service to persons who were not economically dependent, the growth of knowledge of individual behavior—all of these and other influences tended to put social casework in a "treatment focus" and to push into the background the earlier attention to basic social problems. Even during the depression of the 1930s, when social workers such as Harry Hopkins and Frances Perkins were influencing or directing mass programs and thousands of social workers moved into the public services, the movement toward sharpening skills, perfecting techniques, and refining casework processes continued to occupy the attention and energies of the rank and file of the social work profession.

The history of social work has resulted in these two points of view. On the one hand, we have a tradition of social reform and concern with basic social problems; on the other hand, we have translated the modern findings of psychiatry, medicine, and the social sciences into an applied art of social work with individuals and groups. Nathan Cohen has pointed up this problem in his comment: "Modern social work is caught up in this dilemma. With social reform as a mother and psychological individualization as a father, it has difficulty at times in establishing its legitimacy."

These two aspects of social work—practice and policy, psychological individualization and social reform, improvement of individualized services and improvement of social conditions, direct rendering of services and broader programs of prevention, personal therapy and social leadership—can be viewed as a coordinated approach to the solution of those problems, individual and community, with which social work is concerned. These two areas of interest were commented upon by Mary Richmond almost fifty years ago when she said: "The whole of social work is greater than any of its parts. All parts serve personality. . . . Case work serves it by effecting better adjustments between individuals and their social environment . . . social reform serves it by effecting mass betterment through propaganda and social legislation."[8]

As we view the history of the reform movements prior to 1920, we see a social action background in which national associations in the field of welfare were more vigorous than they are today. Nevertheless, we are gradually returning to a period of greater concern with the political and social action scene. The National Association of Social Workers has a Washington office and it testifies regularly upon all welfare matters; the American Public Welfare Association, likewise, has a Washington office; the National Federation of Settlements and Neighborhood Centers has been active in public housing and antipoverty programs; Traveler's Aid has been pressing for assistance to migrants. A most important development is the newly renamed National Assembly for Social Policy and Development, which now comprises some 300 leaders concerned with social policy.

Increasingly, the national associations are recognizing that the great battles of social welfare are being fought in the political arena. One of the positive results of the Social Security Amendments of 1967 was to bring home this fact. At least a score or more of national associations made their views known to Congress.

2. *The national associations as partners of the federal bureaucracy.* It is well known that many national associations are closely related to particular federal agencies. The American Medical Association has had close ties to the United States Public Health Service at various times, sometimes supporting and sometimes opposing its positions. The American Public Welfare Association has been a consistent supporter of public assistance and child welfare programs and its officers have frequently become top federal officials in the Department of Health, Education, and Welfare. The Child Welfare League has had a close tie to the United States Children's Bureau and has promoted its programs.

Perhaps the outstanding example of cooperation between federal agencies and outside groups is provided by the story of the National Institutes of Health. From a relatively small operation a few years ago, the National Institutes of Health has become the world's largest medical research institution. Its growth is due to many factors: the devotion of its staff and its director, Dr. James Shannon; the increasing recognition of national health deficiences; the advance of research techniques; and increased financial resources of the federal government. But a significant factor in its growth has been the zealous and aggressive support of the National Committee

Against Mental Illness and other organizations under the leadership of Mary Lasker, Florence Mahoney, Mike Gorman, and a few noted physicians such as Dr. Howard Rusk, Dr. Michael De Bakey, and Dr. Sidney Farber. Mary Lasker has supported increased appropriations for the National Institutes of Health with as much zeal as Florence Kelley brought to bear on the abolition of child labor—perhaps with more political sophistication and knowledge of political processes. The small group of persons gathered around the nucleus named above (as well as others) have worked closely with Dr. Shannon to promote the National Institutes of Health.[9]

It is well known that each bureaucracy has its own national agency supporters. These relationships are self-evident. Public policy–making in the United States is a decentralized process, and because there is so much decentralization from the Congress to the bureaucracy in Washington, and from Washington to the states and local communities, almost every part of government has a constituency to which it can turn for advice, guidance, and support.

Sometimes the partnership arrangements are questionable to many persons. For example, the national sectarian agencies have frequently demanded representation on official advisory committees in Washington which representation they in fact appoint. In the 1950s, the three major religious groups took the position that two advisory groups—to the Children's Bureau and the Bureau of Public Assistance—should include not merely persons of the religious persuasion of the organization, but persons nominated by the organization. In like manner the American Public Welfare Association has often requested that its representative be present at official meetings of federal and state officials, interjecting a voluntary association into a federal–state relationship activity. The partnership relationships grow increasingly sensitive as public funds to the voluntary agencies become larger and more important. Some child care agencies obtain well over half their income from public welfare departments which pay these agencies for the care of children. Without public funds, some voluntary services would be terminated. When we consider the millions of dollars going to voluntary agencies through Medicare, Medicaid, Hill-Burton funds, vocational rehabilitation programs, child care payments, and a score of other programs, we see a public-voluntary partnership which is significant. The surprising fact is not that national associations are vigorously involved in the partnership but that, considering the financial and philosophical stakes, they are not more active in this area.

It is interesting to note in the context of the frequently expressed fear that federal financing will result in the control of programs or activities that a number of voluntary associations, supported to a great extent by federal funds, have not only been independent and completely free of federal control but frequently have been in opposition to federal policies. Two such associations are the American Public Welfare Association and the National Association for Community Development. The American Public Welfare Association, for example, is financed to a great extent by dues from state and local public welfare departments, and these expenditures are reimbursed by the federal government in accordance with the reimbursement formula in the Social Security Act. As a result, federal funds finance the activities of the APWA, and frequently APWA opposes legislation passed by Congress and occasionally promoted by the executive branch of government.

On the other hand, the increasing receipt of special grants for research and demonstration projects by national agencies might well affect their freedom of action. Can a national organization oppose a federal agency's program when it receives substantial grants from such agency? Does the allure of federal grants make the national voluntary organization more adept at grantsmanship than at politics?

These partnership relations between the bureaucracy and national associations are important in many ways. Such associations can frequently bring nationwide support to the programs of a federal agency; their constituency may be influential with the Congress; and they form a link from those in Washington to a broad constituency. In the "politics of welfare" their support may be a decisive factor.

3. The national voluntary associations in the legislative arena.

Since World War II, national associations have become in-creasingly active in supporting or opposing legislation being considered by the Congress. This increase in legislative activ-ity by national associations involves almost every field of federal government activity. As the federal government ex-panded its peacetime activities after World War II, its influ-ence became all-pervasive; its programs affected the entire economic life of the nation; and changes in federal policy could be decisive in the success or failure of individual enter-prises or community programs. As a result, individuals began to turn more and more to Washington to solve their personal as well as community problems. Finding that group action was an effective method of presenting one's views, individuals pressed for more activity on the part of their national associ-ations or created new ones to lobby for their interests and points of view.

These organizations, representing professions, business groups, scientific organizations, community agencies, and a host of other special interests, did not rely principally on paid lobbyists; rather, they emphasized grass roots pressure, political support, and direct appeal through testimony at hear-ings and through personal contact.

Congress took note of the changing pressures and a Con-gressional committee investigated lobbying at the federal level. This investigation concluded that ". . . the business of influencing legislation is dominated by group effort and that individual activities by persons known as 'lobbyists' are sub-ordinate."[10] The legislative activities of voluntary associations have been extensively studied and documented. They have been effective in the legislative arena for many reasons: they are generally oriented around a specific interest and can focus the energies of their members upon a specific legislative pro-gram which promotes this interest; they are able to influence their members' political behavior; they can utilize large sums of money to promote their legislative activities; and they can frequently mount large-scale nation-wide campaigns to sup-port or oppose legislation. Although there has been very little definitive study of their actual influence, the governmental bureaucracy generally seeks the support of such associations.

Certainly, some of them in the welfare field have had considerable influence. The Townsend movement hastened the action on social security; the voluntary associations were influential in the passage of the 1956 and 1962 service amendments to the Social Security Act; the provision in the 1967 amendments relating to grants for social work education was influenced by pressures from national groups upon officials of the Department of Health, Education, and Welfare and the committees of Congress; telegrams and other representations stimulated by the Citizens Crusade Against Poverty probably assisted in preserving a higher level of appropriations for the Office of Economic Opportunity in 1967.

Looking at the national associations during the past four or five years, four different types of activity in the legislative arena are worth noting:

Legislative objectives. Many organizations publish an annual statement of federal legislative objectives. The most widely disseminated within the social welfare field probably are those of the American Public Welfare Association and the National Association of Social Workers. These objectives have proved useful in focussing membership attention on immediate legislative goals, and enable the association to testify, file statements, and make other representations without the necessity of obtaining approval for specific actions when they are consistent with published objectives.

Information and position statements. An important function of the political process is to keep a constituency informed. Many national voluntary associations in the welfare field do this. The National Association of Social Workers publishes regular communications from its Washington office. Likewise, the American Public Welfare Association has regular publications from Washington keeping its membership abreast of legislative developments. The National Social Welfare Assembly publishes regular information and position statements.

Call to action. Communications to members are a common device to urge action by members in the form of telegrams, letters, and personal representation to the Congress. Practically every important national organization in the welfare field urged its constituency to protest the AFDC amendments of 1967.

Testimony. Increasingly, national welfare associations are testifying at open hearings of Congress. The National Association of

Social Workers testifies several times a year; the American Public Welfare Association almost always appears on public assistance or child welfare matters; the National Social Welfare Assembly (now the National Assembly for Social Policy and Development) has been testifying increasingly in the past few years; and other national groups have appeared or filed testimony. Many persons feel that frequently the national associations' support of public welfare legislation is modest and somewhat cautious. Frequently these national associations file a pro forma statement which puts them on record but which is not as effective as a personal appearance. One study comments that "Private welfare does care about the direction and character of the public welfare program, but its interest is more intellectual than direct. Private agencies have built up a separate clientele with which they are content. Public assistance for the indigent belongs to another world."[11]

What is urgently needed is a comprehensive study of the effectiveness of national welfare associations in the legislative arena. Pending such a study, many observers are convinced that such appearances are important and effective. They build up a valuable legislative record and demonstrate to the Congress that large numbers of people are interested in the particular bill.

4. The national voluntary associations in the administrative and fund allocation process. The experienced welfare "lobbyist" knows that the passage of legislation is only the beginning of the political process. Administrative decisions can forward or retard implementation of the law and lack of financial appropriation can nullify the law.

Much time and effort went into the 1956 amendments to the Social Security Act, which provided additional federal funds to assist the states in meeting the costs of training personnel employed or preparing for employment in public assistance programs. The law was the culmination of several years of diligent effort on the part of officials of the Social Security Administration's Bureau of Public Assistance, the Department of Health, Education, and Welfare, numerous state and local public welfare officials, the APWA, and representatives of the NASW and voluntary agencies. It took a year of intensive work to convince administrative officials in the executive branch of government to adopt the proposal as an official administration recommendation; it took another year to convince Congress. There was the most vigorous discussion and difference of opinion about the federal share: should it be 100 percent, as in some other programs, or 50 percent, as in the federal reimbursement formula for state and local administrative expenses? The compromise was 80 percent.

State and local welfare officials hailed the amendment as a step toward the solution of their manpower problems. Anticipating federal funds, many states drew up plans for staff training and staff development; some appointed staff development personnel; a few received special appropriations or authorization to match the expected money from Washington.

There was one small catch, however: no federal funds were forthcoming. The appropriations committees of Congress refused to appropriate money to make the law operative. The chairman of the House Appropriations Committee did not believe that there was support for such an appropriation from any group but administration officials. The pressures for the enabling legislation died with the enactment of the law; and, in effect, the law died when Congress failed to appropriate money. The failure to allocate funds defeated a long series of rational, significant, and possibly far-reaching administrative decisions.

The interrelationship of administrative decision-making and fund allocation works in reverse fashion also. The 1956 amendments added a section to the Social Security Act which emphasized that the purpose of the Aid to Dependent Children (ADC) program (now known as Aid to Families with Dependent Children—AFDC) was "to help maintain and strengthen family life." In one state, where appropriations for ADC were comparatively adequate, an administrative decision to force recipient mothers to prosecute all deserting fathers without exception may well have resulted in the permanent dissolution of some families, which would have been avoidable if the administrative decision had permitted a case-by-case consideration of exceptions where reunification of the family seemed possible.

Many national agencies, alert to the politics of the congressional arena, are uninformed of and unrelated to administrative policy making. But fund allocation policy is frequently determined by fund allocators through the appropriate process, and national associations need to be more involved in administrative and budgeting decisions if they are to be effective in the political welfare arena. The federal agencies avidly seek support for their efforts to secure adequate appropriations and it is well known that frequently the congressional response to efforts of federal agencies to secure funds depends on the estimate by Congress of the degree to which the federal agency and its program enjoys public favor and support. It is interesting to note how some federal agencies are successful in impressing Congress with their widespread support and therefore with the political risk involved in refusing the agency's request for funds. Commenting on this, one analysis states, "administrators like politicians, must nurse their constituency to insure their survival."

Mention has already been made of the effective support for National Institutes of Health appropriations on the part of a national group. Similar support and testimony have been given by other national associations.

Literature and studies of the politics of administration and fund allocation have been increasing as students of government recognize their importance. Both government agencies and national associations need to develop their cooperative relations in these areas as they have done more effectively in the legislative arena.

5. *National associations as the antagonists of the federal agencies.* Not infrequently the national associations have opposed the proposals of federal agencies. When the Eisenhower Administration took office in 1952, it proposed to limit federal reimbursement to the states for administrative expenses in public assistance. The American Public Welfare Association "killed" the proposal in the Congress. Since the American Public Welfare Association's members and leading officials include state commissioners of welfare, such commissioners enlisted the support of their state governors and congressional representatives in defeating the move. The new administration learned that very little progress can be made in Congress if the American Public Welfare Association vigorously attacks a proposal since this association can usually

corral the Governors behind its position. In the Medicare fight, many national associations opposed the Administration's position; in particular, the American Medical Association, but also the American Dental Association, American Pharmaceutical Association, Blue Cross-Blue Shield, American Farm Bureau Federation, General Federation of Women's Clubs and others. The Elementary Education Bill in 1966 was opposed in part by the American Jewish Congress. For more than a decade, the opposition of the National Conference of Catholic Charities to the proposal by the Department of Health, Education, and Welfare that Child Welfare Services grants to states might be made available for child welfare work in urban areas, effectively prevented the passage of the required legislation by Congress. Unemployment insurance was not extended to hospitals and welfare organizations because of opposition to this by national hospital and welfare associations.

In general, opposition to a legislative proposal by an important national association is usually more effective than its support. The American Public Welfare Association, for example, has supported many proposals which did not become law but rarely is a law passed by Congress to which it is actively opposed.

6. *The national associations as supporters of federal agencies.* As previously indicated, there is a close affiliation of some national associations with specific federal agencies, which lends support to such federal agencies. The AFL-CIO has been a consistent supporter of the housing proposals of the Department of Housing and Urban Development. The National Association of Social Workers and the Council on Social Work Education have supported consistently all proposals by the Department of Health, Education, and Welfare to expand social work education. The Child Welfare League has been a staunch ally of the Children's Bureau, and assisted the Bureau in its unsuccessful efforts to become an independent agency of the Department of Health, Education, and Welfare, responsible to the Secretary of Health, Education, and Welfare.

Frequently, national associations have been in conflict with each other in support of or opposition to an official federal agency position. Thus, in supporting the extension of Federal Child Welfare Services to cities, an ideological battle ensued between the American Public Welfare Association and the National Association of Social Workers on one side and the National Conference of Catholic Charities on the other. The controversy was so bitter as to cause Monsignor O'Grady, the Executive of the National Conference of Catholic Charities to proclaim, "When the proponents of the new public welfare reach their utopia, there will no longer be a place for religion in the American community."[12]

Many national associations claim active participation in federal legislative and administrative matters, but if this is the case, such participation must frequently be a highly kept secret. Of the hundreds of rules promulgated by the Commissioner of Social Security (when the writer occupied the position between 1954–1959)—regulations involving tens of millions of dollars to voluntary agencies and affecting hospitals, nursing homes, homes for unmarried mothers, use of federal funds to purchase voluntary agency services, and many other matters of importance to voluntary effort—only the American Public Welfare Association and the National Conference of Catholic Charities made specific representations on proposed regulations, although many national associations testified on the legislation which was being implemented by such regulations. The test of the effectiveness of national associations in the politics of welfare is the extent to which they influence the political processes—legislative, administrative, judicial.

7. *The national associations as initiators of social policy or programs.* Occasionally, national associations take leadership in initiating social policy changes or programs. Unfortunately, this is not as frequent as it ought to be. Policy makers, both Congressmen and administrative officials, welcome ideas from outside. The Atomic Energy Commission came into being because an informal, ad hoc group of nuclear scientists were alarmed at the possible misuse of atomic energy and they were credited with convincing Congress to set up a civilian authority to control nuclear energy rather than put it under military

control. The consortium of Deans of Schools of Social Work and the national associations which formed a Committee to promote greater federal support for social work education, convinced Federal officials to include this in the Social Security Amendments of 1967. The American Public Welfare Association has initiated several moves to increase federal public assistance grants through convincing the federal agency as to its desirability. The Model Cities legislation was enacted with the assistance of national organizations which stimulated support by local constituents. With so many social problems yet to be solved, the alert national association has unlimited opportunity to initiate and promote new ideas, laws, and programs in the political arena.

8. *The national associations as representatives of special interest groups.* In the politics of welfare the view of national associations is understandably colored by their constituency and special interests. It is to be expected that the National Red Cross would be more interested in federally financed disaster programs than would be the Family Service Association of America, and the National Council on Aging might get more excited about appropriations to the Administration on Aging than would the National Travelers Aid. In some areas where there are no special interest groups, the national associations are not too active. Thus, in public assistance, only the American Public Welfare Association is consistently involved with other voluntary associations becoming active on special issues such as the 1967 Aid to Families with Dependent Children amendments.

Some national associations attempt to stake out a position for specific professions which colors their stance on political questions. The American Medical Association, for example, feels impelled to maintain that only doctors are qualified to judge medical care programs. Testifying before Congress on the National Health Program Bill, the American Medical Association maintained that doctors and doctors alone "were in a position to pass upon the medical side of it, as to the determination of medical care and how to obtain it, and the effect on medical care of the system."

The National Association of Social Workers, although promoting the professional status of the trained social worker and, in the political arena, urging more funds for social work training, nevertheless, "has established itself as a spokesman for many of those served by social workers . . . the social work professional group continues to be regarded as public spokesmen for the relief client."[13]

Some special interest groups among the national associations are particularly effective in the political arena. Mention has already been made of many of them. Perhaps the most numerous and most effective are the Senior Citizens or old-age groups. The aged have become an increasingly active force in the politics of welfare. Undoubtedly their efforts assisted in the passage of Medicare, in increasing Social Security benefits, and in establishing the Administration on Aging.

It is understandable, also, that many national voluntary associations should look upon themselves as the defenders of the voluntary agency—a position which may bring them into conflict with federal agencies on occasion. At times, the huge public programs seem to overwhelm the more restricted voluntary effort. One journal of a national association looked upon the 1962 amendments as infringing upon the exclusive province of the voluntary agency[14] while a prominent social worker urged that government should aid and strengthen those private agencies which perform a valuable service.[15] Protestant welfare leaders have asserted that church welfare services are unique and they recognize deeper needs than public assistance programs, for example.[16]

As a result of the various special interests of national associations, their participation in the politics of welfare is varied and diverse. Almost any welfare issue in the political arena can touch a sensitive chord or specific interest of some national association.

Some New Developments in the Politics of Welfare

Social services under government auspices are undergoing great expansion and change; new ideas command increasing antipoverty programs present new political problems as inattention, threatening to replace or modify existing programs;

digenous residents demand more participation in programs affecting them; and the costs of war continue to cast political shadows over many health and welfare programs.

The politics of welfare is affected by these changes. One hears on all sides that these changes demand greater participation in the political arena. As the President of the Massachusetts Conference of Social Work recently proclaimed: "Our job is in politics—somewhat euphemistically called 'Social Action' by this organization and many others. Our job is to recognize that political action and only political action will bring about the basic, fundamental changes which are necessary. . . ."[17]

New political action groups are also becoming active in politics. Aid to Families with Dependent Children mothers have organized the National Welfare Rights Organization and lobbied against the 1967 AFDC amendments; they are urging a national income guarantee and participating in local, state, and national political activity. The various Urban Coalitions, neighborhood legal services, discussions of negative income tax, and many other organizational and ideological developments—all add to increased interest in the politics of welfare.

Of particular interest is the reorganization of the National Social Welfare Assembly (now the National Assembly for Social Policy and Development) and its possible influence on the political scene. On March 14, 1967, the Assembly adopted a new statement of purpose, function, scope, and structure. The principal purposes of the new organization include voluntary effort to support sound social planning, policies, and programs; to improve governmental and nongovernmental welfare activities; to propose new or changed national social policies and to secure their implementation. Backed by a group of 300 incorporators who represent almost all major national organizations in the welfare field, as well as business, labor, various regions, and other interests, it could, if successful, bring to bear a new and powerful voice in the politics of welfare.

The National Association of Social Workers is also undergoing change in this connection. Although this professional association of social workers has been engaged in various social action and political activities, the membership cries for more effective and meaningful participation in welfare politics. An editorial in the official National Association of Social Workers' journal asserted that social work has professionalized psychological individualization but "when it comes to treating the social situation, we choose to rely upon lay, volunteer initiative in the name of democracy."[18] In December 1967 an influential group within the National Association of Social Workers demanded more meaningful participation of the entire association in social action and urged a closer relationship to emerging urban problems and programs. The Board of Directors of the National Association of Social Workers has taken steps to further these desires.

The Urban Coalition has presented a new development which bids fair to becoming increasingly important. Urban Coalition is a response to the recognition that our system is not working effectively. Businessmen are questioning present programs and efforts and the Urban Coalition movement is bringing business leaders into the politics of welfare.

Conclusion

This discussion has attempted to highlight a few facets of the subject "Federal Agencies, National Associations, and the Politics of Welfare." Mention has been made of the growing importance of government welfare programs; the significance of control of government welfare programs and national associations by a relatively few persons; the importance of administrative decisions and fund allocations by federal officials; the proliferation of voluntary national associations; the national association as promoter, reformer, and initiator of public social policies and programs; the growing partnership between the national associations and federal agencies; the work of national associations in federal legislation and fund allocations, and as supporters and antagonists of the federal bureaucracy; the national associations as special interest groups, and some of the newer developments influencing the politics of welfare.

As we view the central domestic social problems of our society—poverty, race, ghetto slums, and related problems—there is a growing realization on the part of national associations that their contributions must be made increasingly through politics. One of the serious problems of American society is that of social alienation or the distance between the individual and his society. Perhaps the national associations, many of which have roots in every community, can assist in bridging this gap and bringing to officials in Washington the viewpoints of their grass roots constituents. In a sense, the large number of national associations constitutes a guarantee that persons and organizations outside of government will be participating in the politics of welfare, and it is to be hoped that the national association–federal agency partnership will grow ever stronger. Many problems of concern today can be solved if the private welfare sector and government agencies work together in the political process.

NOTES

1. National Social Welfare Assembly, *Joint Statement On Welfare Policy*, November 15, 1967.
2. Telegram to President Johnson from the President of the National Association of Social Workers.
3. One of the few comprehensive attempts to study this phenomenon is Gilbert Y. Steiner, *Social Insecurity: The Politics of Welfare* (Chicago: Rand McNally, 1966).
4. For a comprehensive review of this period, see Charles A. Chambers, *Seedtime Of Reform* (Ann Arbor: University of Michigan Press, 1st ed. Ann Arbor Paperback, 1967).
5. *Ibid.*, pp. 22–23.
6. *Hammer v. Dagenhart*, 247 U.S. 251, 38 Sup. Ct. 529 (1918).
7. Nathan E. Cohen, *Social Work in the American Tradition* (New York: Holt, 1958), p. 103.
8. Mary E. Richmond, *What Is Social Case Work?* (New York: Russell Sage Foundation, 1922), p. 259.
9. For an interesting account of this relationship, see Elizabeth Brenner Drew, "The Health Syndicate/Washington's Noble Conspirators," *The Atlantic* (December 1967), 75–82.
10. U.S. Congress, House, Committee on Lobbying Activities, *Report and Recommendations on Federal Lobbying Act*, 81st Cong., 2nd Sess., 1951, Rept. 3239, p. 3.

11. Steiner, *Social Insecurity*, p. 12.
12. U.S. Congress, House, Committee on Ways and Means, Hearings, *Social Security Legislation*, 88th Cong., 2d Sess., 1958, p. 828.
13. Steiner, *Social Insecurity*, p. 204.
14. "Who Has The Answer," *Catholic Charities*, 46 (June 1962), 2.
15. Bernard Coughlin, S. J., "Private Welfare in a Public Welfare Bureaucracy," *Social Service Review* (June 1961), 192.
16. Rev. G. S. Thompson, *The New York Times*, February 11, 1965.
17. Speech delivered by Mrs. Oliver Cope to the Massachusetts Conference of Social Work, Boston, Massachusetts, November 30, 1967.
18. Robert Morris (Editorial), *Social Work*, October 1964, p. 2.

10 ALAN D. WADE

On Humanizing
the Bureaucracies

Dean Schottland, out of his own distinguished background of scholarship and statemanship in social welfare, has ably presented a comprehensive description of the interplay of bureaucratic and political forces at the federal level in the enactment of present social welfare policy. It is a scholarly and an accurate picture of the way things have been with the welfare state. The problem is that the way things have been with our welfare system, and with our nation, provides us with little or no help in settling the current turmoil in our nation, in designing the kinds of social institutions required by the good society of the future, and in developing the new political forms needed to get us there somewhat intact. These observations, therefore, do not criticize Dean Schottland's analysis, but raise some questions about the future that his analysis forces upon us.

First, is "the welfare state" itself a goal that ought to be supported? Dean Schottland observes: "No one doubts that we have a welfare state and most critical observers do not question the conclusion that the welfare state is here to stay. . . ." Perhaps we ought to begin to question whether the welfare state represents an adequate conception for the society

This chapter is a response to the preceding chapter by Charles I. Schottland.

of the future. If it is here to stay, do we really want it, or does its very meaning reflect an archaic social philosophy?

Our students these days have a habit of cutting through to the central issue. The student newspaper at the University of Michigan reported on Secretary Cohen's April 1968 honors convocation address on the Ann Arbor campus. According to the report, a large banner reading "HEW: THE WELFARE FIGLEAF ON THE WARFARE STATE" was unfurled and held up to view during the secretary's speech. Harvey Wheeler in "The Politics of Revolution" expresses the same thought in different words, suggesting that the welfare states rests "upon militarism and imperialism abroad and cultural despotism at home."[1] This view of the welfare state takes note of the creation of an underclass systematically alienated from participation in the public life of America, including participation in the decisions regarding its welfare which Mr. Schottland so clearly describes as made by an establishment elite of bureaucrats, politicians, and professionals.

The view of the welfare state as anachronism reflects two other factors in the current scene: (1) the use of the welfare state as an actual instrument of domestic oppression; and (2) the link-up between our American efforts to impose our beliefs on people abroad through main force and our subjugation of our poor at home.

In the ghettos of our big cities, welfare workers, along with police, storekeepers, and landlords' agents, are regarded by the people as immediate oppressors—as the most obvious and available representatives of a society whose affluence they see on their ten-dollar television screens, but which stands in their way at every step. The rural poor in many ways lead different lives from their city brothers and sisters, but here, again, "the welfare" is seen more often than not as an oppressive force—one that, for example, can manipulate them into virtually forced labor at low wages according to the needs of local government and agriculture.

Perhaps the most dramatic evidence of the use of the welfare state by local government as a means of oppression is noted in the 1967 report to the Field Foundation regarding

starvation among children in Mississippi, prepared by a panel
of eminent pediatricians and other physicians:

> We saw children who are hungry and who are sick—children for
> whom hunger is a daily fact of life and sickness, in many forms,
> an inevitability. We do not want to quibble over words, but "mal-
> nutrition" is not quite what we found; the boys and girls we saw
> were hungry—weak, in pain, sick; their lives are being shortened;
> they are, in fact, visibly and predictably losing their health, their
> energy, their spirits. They are suffering from hunger and disease
> and directly or indirectly they are dying from them—which is
> exactly what starvation means.[2]

What these physicians are referring to is genocide, the conscious effort of local and state government to destroy a race
of people. In this instance, we are not viewing the failure of
the idea of the welfare state to be applied efficiently. We are
viewing, instead, its efficient use as an engine for the destruction of human beings.

Exploitation of the poor in the United States inevitably
becomes linked with their exploitation in other parts of the
world. The civil rights movement and the poor people's campaign in the United States represent one segment of the
demands of people all over the world for an end to the famine
that hovers over the heads of most of them, for a redistribution
of the world's material resources, and for a share in the
decision-making power to see that these things are done. Our
own ability to deal effectively with hunger and oppression at
home—to put into effect that kind of cooperation in government that Dean Schottland suggests is so necessary—is of
course almost completely paralyzed at the present time by the
focus of our national will and vast material resources on a
single end. I refer, of course, to the vicious war in Vietnam,
where we seem hellbent on the destruction of an entire people
on the incredible grounds that we must make it possible for
what we call democracy to be preserved there. This crime
committed in the name of democracy is, then, the American
response to the world revolution of rising expectations. And
we use the fantastic expenses in money and manpower which

it requires to justify our inability to provide jobs, housing, food, and new social institutions so that our own poor may become a part of our society.

In addition to the question concerning the adequacy of the welfare state as we have known it as a goal for our society, brief attention must be given to one other basic point made by Dean Schottland—namely, the "realization that government is the province of the few." In general, it is probably true that most people are not interested in government and in politics. The view he presents seems indeed to be an accurate one—i.e., the complex of programs making up the welfare state has developed largely in response to the interests and commitments of an elite bureaucracy in government usually supported by their counterparts in a variety of national associations. The question for us is not whether such a view accurately depicts the past. What must trouble us is: How can we go about breaking up such an unholy alliance so that the needs of our people can be gratified, and so that our nation can get moving again?

There is much of "politicking," horsetrading, logrolling, compromising, and temporizing in Dean Schottland's quite accurate presentation of the welfare world as we have known it, but nothing of politics or planning in the Aristotelian sense. There is, in short, no evidence that those who "cooperate" in the development of plans for other people have a clearly articulated ideology, a guiding sense of the relationship of one program to another, or a sound view of human life cycle needs. Aristotle in his *Ethics and Politics* repeatedly returns to ethical considerations as the fundamental companion of the art of governing, pointing out that "The state came into being for the sake of life, but it exists for the sake of the good life."

Obviously, there is a problem with our democracy. At the very time in history when people are demanding opportunities for participation in a creative and *affective* life, power is becoming more centralized—in Dean Schottland's example, in the welfare agencies and their bedfellows among the national associations. Harvey Wheeler in the article referred to previously describes the crisis of direct democracy:

It occurs when societies become so complex that their administration requires expert technical knowledge in addition to practical wisdom. When this happens, there begins to appear what might be called an informal technological despotism. Society is divided into those with the technological prerequisites for exercising political office and those without.[3]

He goes on to point out that a process of conversion of democracy into despotism occurs, in which representative democracy becomes transformed into political alienation. The tragedy is that the more complex society becomes, the more important it is that political power be spread widely throughout the population.

What is needed is a new conception of community, a truly revolutionary conception in which political power is spread, a variety of responses will be encouraged from individuals and groups in the running of different aspects of community life, and the new science and technology will be enlisted in a new ecological view of human life that bends social institutions to the biological and affective needs of man. Perhaps, what is required is a dedication to taming the rampant bureaucracies of which most of us are a part, humanizing them, and transforming them into sensitive instruments for enlisting people, including our clients, in the process of planning for the good society.

NOTES

1. Harvey Wheeler, "The Politics of Revolution," *The Center Magazine*, I: 3 (March 1968), 53.
2. Milton J. E. Senn, M.D., Robert Coles, M.D., et al. "Children in Mississippi," A Report to the Field Foundation, mimeographed, June 1967.
3. Wheeler, "Politics of Revolution," p. 62.

11 | TOM HAYDEN

Colonialism and Liberation
as American Problems

In July 1967, one week after the Newark uprising, I wrote: "This country is experiencing its fourth year of urban revolt, yet the message from Newark is that America has learned almost nothing since Watts."

There is no reason to revise that conclusion today.

America is nearly bankrupt in its ability to find social, economic or political answers to racism. The "solutions" being prepared are increasingly military ones.

If there are no answers, it is because men concentrate on the wrong questions. We should abandon the notions that America is a melting pot, that the welfare state is progressive, that revolution is impossible because black people are a minority. We must look at America as a new and violent form of colonial society, and we must draw the consequences.

America as a Colonial Society

There are three continual objections made to the use of *colonialism* as a term to describe the ghetto conditions in the United States. The first is that black people are nationalized Americans, not people of a separate identity governed by a foreign power. The second is that the Constitution supports equal citizenship for all people rather than a principle of second-class status. The third is that racism is based in historical prejudice rather than economic profit. Each of these objections contains an important point. Taken together they make it necessary to go beyond the traditional definition of colonialism as a system of economic exploitation based on political control of one people by another. But they do not erase the essential similarities between American racism and the colonialism of the Western European powers. America is a colonial society in a new sense.

Let us examine the objections to using the term *colonialism.*

Objection 1: *that black people are American, not foreign.* In the obvious sense of "citizenship" no one can dispute this assertion. However it is assumed mistakenly that black people are an assimilated people like the European immigrants who were integrated into the American society. The falseness of this view is obvious. The African slaves did not choose to live in America as did the immigrants; they were forcibly taken here. Once here, the chattel slavery system violated their family structure and culture, while the Europeans, on the other hand, drew their greatest strength from the traditions they preserved. With the passing of slavery, black people faced a permanent situation of underemployment, while the Europeans moved into a system of expanding economic opportunities. And, of course, the policy of discrimination was a deterrent against progress which the Europeans faced in a far milder and less universal sense than the "emancipated" blacks. Thus the separate status of black people in the midst of American society has always been a fact. That black people identify themselves as Americans, that they express loyalty to the country as a whole, should blind no one to the essential differences between their experience and that of the more assimilated white immigrants. The nationalist concept of blacks as "overseas Africans" refers to an important reality which the concept of the "melting pot" fails to explain.

Objection 2: *black people have equal consitutional rights with whites.* As with the first objection, no one can disagree that there is a significant difference between this constitutional reality and that of colonial societies where entire classes are disenfranchised. Yet no one can deny that the constitutional promise has never materialized for black people as a whole

class. Legal barriers to voting and other forms of social participation, presumably outlawed by the Constitution itself, are
still the subject of heated controversy in the southern states
and part of the North. When looked at from a wider perspective than that of technical rights, moreover, there appears a
systematic pattern of underrepresentation of black people in
every decision-making sphere that affects their lives. Tenants
in slum housing or federally constructed public housing projects have no meaningful power over their rents or living
conditions. Mothers on welfare have no meaningful voice over
the administration and rules governing them. The citizen of
the ghetto has no meaningful procedure for deterring police
abuse. Black workers are employed in conditions—for example,
domestic work—which offer few opportunities for unioniza-
tion. The possession of the vote is of little value in offsetting
these denials of power over one's life. Having 10 percent of
the votes in a system of institutionalized racism guarantees
nothing.

Objection 3: *the black population in America is not a source
of raw materials and cheap labor in the way that colonized
peoples are.* Certainly the slaves were brought here as cheap
labor, and after "emancipation" blacks have been under-
employed so consistently that we must suppose our competitive economic system needs a degree of joblessness. However,
it also is possible to view the black population as surplus or
irrelevant manpower, a view from which alarming conclusions
can be drawn. In the old forms of colonialism, brutality rarely
became genocidal because the colonialist needed the slaves for
production; but in a new form in which slaves are economically useless, what is to prevent genocide when the colonialist
becomes irritated by the slaves' demands?

These objections in no way change the fact that black
people, as a group, are blocked from participating in the
"mainstream" of American society. They live and work
within frameworks established by the racial majority. They
are subjected to a combination of racism and economic exploitation. This is the substance of a colonial situation although the forms are distinctly American.

Beyond Traditional Solutions

One implication of this perspective is that solutions to the problem will not be of a traditional kind. The channels of mobility open to the white immigrants are closed to black people. Certainly, of course, there are opportunities to rise in the economic system for the black individual but not for his social group as a whole. The individual who "succeeds" usually does so in terms entirely defined by the white community. He becomes a token or marginal person in an alien system, losing his identification with a group of his own. The long-term solution, viewed from this perspective, would be culturally genocidal: blacks would have to become "whites" in all respects to gain majority acceptance. But this is clearly impossible—no amount of adaptation to majority standards changes the color of skin. Stokely Carmichael points out that black people *have* adapted to the Puritan ethic—that hard work brings personal reward—but generations of labor in the cotton fields brought no gains. If the Protestant Ethic were true for all, black people would be millionaires. The problems of black people are not individual problems. The problems are collective. Self-help cannot build houses, schools, hospitals, or modernize whole urban areas. These problems require structural change and public resources.

The other common avenue of change in America, besides individual entrepreneurship, is pressure-group politics. This too can be of value to individuals and, at certain times, to the group as a whole. Wage increases, housing reform, city services, due process of law can all be achieved to some extent. Veto power can be achieved, as well, to prevent discriminatory laws, rent increases, welfare cuts, certain political abuses. The problem is that the achievements are impossible to make secure in a racist colonial society. The period of Reconstruction is the best historical example of this reversal of gains. But the 1960s are full of new examples. The Mississippi Freedom Democratic Party in 1964 was the most representative group of black Mississippians ever organized, yet they were rejected in their bid for representation by the decision of the national Democratic Party. Adam Clayton Powell is one of the most popular congressmen in the country, yet he was stripped of his rank by the decision of the Congress. Any organized black force, if it fights according to the traditions of pressure groups, finds itself only able to make temporary coalitions with different elements in the majority. Other pressure groups have succeeded in their aims because they were able to incorporate themselves into the dominant society. Black people cannot be incorporated in the same way.

Nor can the situation be changed by the federal government or by national coalitions of business, labor, the churches and other groups. The interests of these groups cannot coincide with the interests of ghetto dwellers. Investment in the slums, as even David Rockefeller admits, is a bad business risk. The alternative—planned development under government direction—is opposed as socialism. The main reason elites are now concerned with the slum is the need to maintain "order," which means the essentials of an institutional system that excludes black people as a group. Influential groups may support reforms of a minor kind within this framework of order, either from a sense of humanitarianism or a desire to maintain the system as a whole. Thus a welfare and unemployment insurance program has been adopted, individual rights tend to be respected, groups are permitted a wide freedom to peacefully protest injustices, and occasionally token material improvements are made in housing or other fields.

The value of these liberties and welfare state reforms should not be underestimated, but the greater danger in America is in the exaggeration of their scale. The priorities of the majority, and the reason that black people cannot count on that majority, are revealed sharply in attitudes toward the welfare state. The average white taxpayer typically feels that his earnings are being poured out in support of the "shiftless" underclass, but does not object to the fact that, in reality, nearly all his taxes go toward the expansion of the military establishment. In large measure the American welfare state is a myth. The people at the bottom tend to survive because America is prosperous, not because it is just. The decay of our cities, a process stretching over generations, is the most

visible symptom of basic social injustice and neglect. That
dangerous housing, inadequate schools and medical facilities
should exist in a society as wealthy as this one demonstrates
the feebleness of welfare.

White Response to Black Protest

The people with fewest illusions about the welfare state
are the poor who are served by it. When they protest, usually
in the name of recognized American ideals, an interesting
reaction follows. Some among the majority react sympathetically, though not always with real understanding of the
causes. But a sufficient number of opposing interests are
aroused to prevent any drastic change, and often even moderate changes are blocked. The poor, who in most cases begin
by politely petitioning their governors, soon take more dramatic steps, thinking they can perhaps awaken the conscience
of the majority or at least of higher authorities. They do
awaken the conscience of some people, and to some extent
they force elites to concede token changes. But at the same
time, a "counterrevolution" is triggered against the potential
of revolution which has been seen in the mounting protest.
The system as a whole becomes deadlocked. No more than
token reforms, crumbs, result for the protestors. The scale of
their protest increases as they realize that appeals to conscience
are inadequate. They look for methods of transcending the
rules of pressure politics which have not worked. They begin
civil disobedience and disruption. The immediate reaction of
the power structure is to maintain order. The police are
brought into the conflict. Considerations of social, economic,
or political solutions to the conflict gradually are replaced by
the emphasis on law and order. Violent repression becomes
routine.

This pattern is concretely illustrated by events in Newark
during the last year. Official Newark, the business and political
elite, had documented reports on the magnitude of poverty in
the city long before the rebellion of July 1967. The power
structure knew, too, that it was "sitting on a powder keg."
Yet those in power could not and would not make changes.

When the revolt finally occurred, there were no further references by officials to the long-standing injustice at the root of the problem. The only question for officials was that of "law and order." The police, guardsmen, and troopers went to work. It was legitimate to shoot looters after calling "halt." Policemen carried their private guns into the battle (then there could be no official ballistics check later). Sniping incidents were fabricated. Mass arrests were made. Newark fell under military occupation.

In the wake of the rebellion Governor Hughes took no action but appointed a commission. Its report ultimately was critical of police behavior and of Newark's political insensitivity, though in the framework of calling for a more rational system of putting down rebellions. Not only was the report modest, but the commission was without legislative power to implement its proposals. Yet the report was explosive enough to make Governor Hughes suppress it after printing 4,000 copies and refuse publication rights to a paperback company. In the meantime, the County Grand Jury investigating the 26 killings that occurred in the rebellion returned only one indictment—on a black man for supposedly shooting a black woman. John Smith, the cabdriver whose brutal beating by the police triggered the rebellion, was found guilty in Municipal Court of having assaulted the police officers. The Newark Police Department has been exonerated, has received $250,000 in City Council appropriations for additional weapons and has hooked up informally with an armed white vigilante organization from an Italian ward.

The same process is apparent at the national level, especially in the events following the assassination of Martin Luther King. The immediate worry of the power structure was not that America was a violent and sick society, but that blacks would rebel at the slaying of their leader. Despite the Vietnam war and the annual 80 billion dollars spent for defense, despite the massive preparation of police for the coming summer, despite the repeated killing of civil rights leaders, President Johnson could still implore the black people not to follow the road of "blind violence." The bankruptcy of America was most exposed in the fact that no major leader dared express anger at the killing of King, for there was nothing to do with anger but burn. No demonstration was going to change policy, just as King's demonstrations had not before. The "constructive ways" had been tried before and failed; now there was no "constructive outlet" for rage left. This bankruptcy was proven most finally in the "civil rights" legislation that Congress passed as a tribute to Dr. King. The law is known euphemistically as an "open housing law" but in reality it is a fantastic police-state plan. The open housing provisions are meaningless because sufficient legislation is on the books from Reconstruction, because the procedures for complaint read like an obstacle course, because only 80 percent of housing is covered, and even then it is covered only in stages until 1970. The other provisions of the act are unreported and more lethal:

1. the civil rights protection part does not cover economic intimidation;
2. interfering with the operation of a store during a riot becomes a felony;
3. teaching how to make an explosive device with reason to know it might be used in a riot becomes a felony;
4. interfering with firemen or policemen during a riot becomes a felony, and all law enforcement personnel are made exempt from prohibitions against violating the civil rights of citizens;
5. a riot is defined as a public disturbance involving three or more people together with either an act or threat of violence (so it becomes a crime to defend rebellion as a right);
6. the penalties for any of the above are more severe than those which might be imposed on a realtor if he is found guilty of discrimination in the sale of housing.

The trend is clear. During times of relative social peace, the issue of race goes unresolved. When the issue is forced by black people for reasons of dignity and survival, the answer is to suspend politics and restore order. When the streets are occupied by troops the ultimate colonial substance of the system is revealed.

Foreign Policy Reflects Colonial Purpose

American foreign policy differs very little in essentials from the domestic colonial policy. In the Third World a very clear pattern stands out. In countries where there is thorough-going corruption and poverty, the United States is doing little more than developing the "infrastructure" of transportation routes which makes American business expansion more efficient. Foreign aid, opposed as "charity," is defended primarily as insurance against revolution. The greatest American aid goes to countries which are unstable because of insurgent or revolutionary movements. Invariably this aid is military in character, doing little if anything about the underlying social crises. In countries where a revolutionary movement threatens to replace pro-Western ruling elites, the United States intervenes with force. In all of these cases, the problems of poverty and underdevelopment are not considered from the viewpoint of injustice and social need, but from the viewpoint of U.S. strategic interests. These interests now are counterrevolutionary.

What has happened in Vietnam is a perfect case of this pattern evolving. After considering whether it could replace the French in the Southeast Asian "sphere of influence" in the 1940s, the U.S. decided to supply money and arms to help the French reconquer Vietnam from the victorious Vietminh. Following the defeat of the French at Dienbienphu and the Geneva Accords, the U.S. chose and backed the reactionary Diem dictatorship in South Vietnam. Diem was supplied with weapons and his police administration was modernized. In addition, "social reform" was proposed as a method of stabilizing the regime. But the reforms proposed actually consituted a counterrevolution in the literal sense of the word. American aid personnel proposed retitling landlords to property taken from them in the revolutionary war, then offering rent control and credit to the peasants. Even if the American-inspired programs had been more realistic, they would have failed—as they continue to fail today—because the U.S. sought reforms while restoring the old order of mandarins who had already lost the revolution. The U.S. chose the preservation of order rather than the risk of reforms which might alienate the most solid anticommunists and entrenched bureaucrats. The result, of course, was not order but the escalation of force in a futile effort to establish order. Today we are witnessing an extreme form of the basic pattern: the gradual destruction of Vietnam as a society because the Vietnamese will not accept the American prescription for their development.

This is essentially the same policy that prevails in American ghettos, carried to a destructive extreme: In the beginning, a long period of neglect while the poor struggle as second-class humans; then the initiation of protest, followed by the mixture of palliatives and violence. Then insurrection. Frenzied counterrevolution. Finally: Promises of a Great Society, in Asia and Harlem, after the napalming. Doves and hawks are part of the same system.

Revolutionary Consciousness

The evidence is growing that the only way out of underdevelopment is through revolution.

The haves will not help the have-nots. Those who have (money, status, security, privilege) define what they have as limited. There is not enough to go around, they think, no matter if we are the richest country in the world. In addition, there is a sense of guilt, of having stolen someone else's property, a sense that there will be debts to pay if the rebels (the blacks, the yellows) take over. The haves may be right. An entire system, of international proportions, is at stake. It is an empire of property, of military machinery, of political domination. When protest begins, the haves draw together sufficiently to prevent effective reform. The have-nots are left to choose between submission and more militant protest. There is no basis for hope unless the struggle is begun.

There is no way to begin the struggle unless what Oscar Lewis calls "the culture of poverty" is thrown off. This is the mood of despair, the sense of personal ineffectiveness, the loss of morale and self-esteem which, in Lewis' view, seems to be characteristic of the poor in colonial and certain capitalist societies. This culture, which appears to the privileged class as a sign of innate inferiority and laziness, grips a people threatened with the loss of identity and decision-making power to superior forces. The only apparent way to break out of the culture is not by copying the terms of the dominant, stultifying culture, but by rebellion. The act of rebellion requires a new appraisal of self, a rejection of the dominant cultural styles in behalf of more authentic or natural ones. It requires a realization that the blame for poverty falls not on oneself but on others who are responsible. It requires a sense that misery is not the result of God's inscrutable will but the result of a concrete power structure's priorities. The act of rebellion is the beginning of a man's making history and the end of his being its object.

We are witnessing this process in the ghettos. There is an order, a logic, about the seemingly-chaotic "riots" taking place in most American cities. American society has had its chance to solve the racial problem in the context of peace, and failed. Hard puritan work has failed. Petitions, organized lobbying, voting, and demonstrations have failed. The civil rights leadership—good moral men seeking to make America's words and laws take effect—has failed. Suddenly, however, people jam the streets. The people commit revolutionary violence, primarily against property. Their act is selective and concrete: to steal back some material goods from the society which has stolen from them. The act is profoundly unifying for the community, and a sense of power and pride runs through a majority of the people. The police violence naturally causes fear and intimidation, but also hatred and shock. Things will never be the same again. A sense of self-determination is born. Those who believe this is simply an aggressive desire to have what white Americans have should recall that the first American revolutionaries believed they were fighting for their rights as Englishmen.

The Relevance of Race

Many will agree that development of a revolutionary consciousness to replace the "culture of poverty" is desirable, but will ask: What kind of revolution, indeed what kind of change

at all, can a group make which is irrelevant to economic production and counts for only 10 percent of the population?
Revolutions can only be made by groups that are relevant to
the social structure they wish to change; because black people
are marginal economically and numerically, what is their
relevance?

The answer is that black people may very well have the
power to destroy America's position in the world. America is
looking for trade opportunities and other forms of influence
in a world in which colored nations are assuming power. Dean
Rusk himself once acknowledged (before the Vietnam war)
that the American racial crisis is the country's leading foreign
policy problem. As long as there remains the racial crisis, U.S.
foreign policy will be looked upon as hypocritical. Allied nations will lack confidence about the stability of America's
future. The U.S. will be overextended; unable to find the resources to deal with crises around the world and at home.
And black organizations here will find increasing support for
their struggle—and opposition to suppression—from nations
of the "third world." The black minority at home is part of
a colored majority in the world.

But black people occupy a relevant position inside the
American social structure as well. The "sharpest contradiction" in this situation, as it takes shape at home, is between
the oppressed and concentrated people of the ghettos and
the centers of commerce they surround. If black people
follow the road of the last few summers, they can do im-
mense damage to some of America's most vital institutions.
The cities are the "jungles" in which armed guerrilas, with
popular support, can carry out disruption of commerce and
communication with great success. The climate of terror
created is already driving greater numbers of whites from the
cities, abandoning them to the growing black populations.
With coordinated nationwide attacks a total social crisis of
unprecedented scale could be created within a few years.

The other possibility is that the period of spontaneous rebellion will lead into a more organized and political period.
The failure of the government to deliver change, the violence of the police, and other signs of American racism, are

showing black people the need for unity and struggle in a more concrete way than any nationalist ideology could do. It is likely that united political organizations of a coalition character will develop in urban areas. These will be more or less militant depending on leadership and local conditions. They will serve as institutional centers for protest and service in the community. They will teach people organizing skills and will develop programs for change. Their emphasis might vary—organization of tenants, welfare mothers, youth groups, educational workshops, or electoral campaigns—but they will have a grassroots, black power orientation. They will be supported and sometimes staffed by black students—now the most revolutionary leadership group—from nearby campuses.

If there is success in the search for independent political power, such power could be used to gain resources through taxation, building up voting power for bargaining purposes and developing police power as a deterrent to white racism. There would be a possibility of bargaining for change without bargaining away independence.

Having pointed out these possibilities, it is important to add that there is no inevitability about the development of revolutionary change. A "new deal" welfare expansion for blacks, within the framework of imperialism, may still be worked out through a combination of pressures and material rewards. For example, governmental and business leaders, seeing the threat, may move to reorganize city boundaries to prevent black political majorities. This would be an unspoken consequence of plans to reconstitute cities as planned metropolitan areas. The difficulty in achieving such an alteration, however, should not be underestimated. Much as various sophisticated planners desire metropolitan reorganization, their dreams are exactly contrary to those of the white suburbanites. The suburbanites, having left the cities to avoid their crises, will not be easily persuaded that they should be reintegrated into a metropolitan area with a large black population.

The other possible means of softening the crisis, more achievable in the short run, is through business and foundation support of moderate black political leaders. This seems to have happened in Cleveland and perhaps Gary. In Cleveland the downtown business community, linked with the Ford Foundation, supported a civil rights campaign that elected a black Mayor. The new Mayor, however, tends to represent the interests of the black and white middle class, professional, and commercial communities. He opposes insurrection. He supported the Johnson Administration, and the Vietnam war, presumably expecting to win federal funds for Cleveland. This "containment" strategy is faced with enormous obstacles: the indifference of the Congress to ghetto needs, the lack of incentive for business to invest in the slums, the lack of other black or white power groups with whom Mayor Stokes might ally. If the strategy fails to deliver concrete changes, as it no doubt will, the result will be a more explosive ghetto. Time will have been gained, people's sense of expectation will have increased, but a solution will not have been found.

Some expect that the most likely scenario of the future is neither revolution nor partial reform, but a repression which would set back all opportunities for change. Part of this view is that the white power structure should not be provoked by mass rioting or threats of violence. This fear of repression has been invoked by moderates at every new stage of the civil rights movement since 1960. There has been repression and political intimidation at every new point of development, but never sufficient to prevent the movement's growth. Undoubtedly the U.S. desire to keep a democratic image contributes to its hesitation in repressing insurgents. Moreover, there are divisions of opinion in high circles over the effectiveness of repression—whether, for instance, Stokely Carmichael would be more important as a martyr in jail than as an agitator in the streets. There are practical risks which befall repressors also. If black resistance grew against the occupying police, the cities might have to be destroyed or become permanently insecure.

No rebel wants repression in the beginning. He prefers a legal and peaceful method of change. But the characteristic of a rebel is that he does not give up if such change is blocked. He finds new forms. His beliefs are too deep to surrender.

He insists on the ultimate legality of his actions—as expressed in the Declaration of Independence—even if at present he goes to jail for them. He risks repression without welcoming it.

A Program of Self-Determination

Those who fear repression tend to lecture militants when they should be proving with deeds that meaningful change can be accomplished within the present framework of society. From a theoretical viewpoint, America seems to possess the wealth and constitutional flexibility necessary to permit change to occur in a relatively peaceful way. The question is whether it is possible to define a set of goals that are achievable without requiring an immediate transformation of American society, but at the same time goals consistent with the need to liberate the society from racism. The simplest way of stating the goals and the issues is: Can self-determination for black people be created even partially within the framework of American society?

There has been confusion—legitimate as well as the breast-beating variety—on the meaning of "self-determination." A narrow perspective has assumed that only two outcomes of the black-white struggle are possible, integration or separation. But neither of these concepts has clear meaning now. The issue now is power, the idea that black people should control the communities and institutions which now control them. This emphasis points toward certain goals, among them:

- Predominantly black political parties
- Black labor organizations or caucuses within unions
- Cultural institutions developing awareness of Afro-American history; participation in control of ghetto schools by parents, teachers and students
- *Abolition of the social work profession;* recognition of "welfare rights" unions as bargaining agents in matters pertaining to the scale and administration of public assistance
- Public housing administered and owned by a combination of tenants and community housing corporations
- Reduction or abolition of private absentee ownership of housing;

in the interim, establishment of tenant unions with recognized
powers to negotiate contracts and grievances; initiation of individual and collective ownership of housing by residents themselves

- Community control of police; elected civilian review boards in
  each precinct with powers to investigate, subpoena, and initiate
  proceedings for the removal of officers or changes in department
  policy
- Establishment of cooperatively owned stores; management of
  national chain stores by local business associations; taxation of
  chain stores for community needs.

This emphasis in no way underestimates the need for money
from the government as part of the solution. Rather the issue
of funding should be seen in a new perspective. The present
public expeditures for "welfare" are not only too small but,
more important, are administered through a machinery which
perpetuates colonial domination. The idea of self-determination, however, supposes that new institutions must be constructed, from the bottom up, before funds can be distributed
according to need. Undoubtedly, this institutional change in
the ghetto would have broad national effects. For instance,
some form of national economic planning would necessarily
come into effect.

This perspective is not utopian. The logic of the present
crisis points towards the eventual adoption of these changes
out of necessity. The present administrative machinery of the
ghetto is being challenged and undermined. Most police departments find it difficult to recruit new men; many policemen are departing the ghettos to take safer jobs with fire
departments or county government. Caseworkers are equally
difficult to recruit; they fear going into the "field" and in
many places are not insured by their employers later than
midafternoon. The same pressures affect teachers in ghetto
schools; they fear the students and the hostile ghetto. Landlords now take physical risks by attempting to collect rent
from angry tenants. City services in general are becoming
impossible to manage.

A more repressive machinery would be useless. The tension
between people and the agencies would increase, and re-

cruiting, management problems, and costs would multiply. A more "modern" administrative approach—creating higher wages and incentives for personnel to staff the current machinery—is not working where it is being tried. There are safer jobs which pay as well. The more liberal elements of ghetto administration, such as VISTA and antipoverty agencies, are also in crisis. People who want to "fight City Hall" are blocked or weeded out, leaving control in the hands of mediocre antipoverty careerists dependent on the local government.

There is no way out of the impasse except through structural change. Reform cannot be administered by reactionaries. The beginning of a solution requires power to be exercised by the community.

The White Community: Transcending Guilt

Camus and Sartre have asked: Can a man condemn himself? Can whites, particularly liberal whites, condemn themselves? Can they stop blaming blacks and start blaming their own system? *Are they capable of the shame which might become a revolutionary emotion?*

—*Stokely Carmichael*

A new perspective is required of white Americans:

First, America must be seen as a colonial society, not a melting pot in which integration can be realized.

Second, the issue of race is an issue of self-determination.

Third, self-determination cannot be "granted." It always is wrested from those who oppose it. People first win self-determination, then their former oppressors "grant" it.

Fourth, the battle for self-determination is long or short, peaceful or bloody, according to the degree of vested interest and determination of the oppressors. It is possible, theoretically at least, for a process of challenge-and-concession to gradually cripple racism with a minimum of destruction to the framework of due process and law.

Fifth, the establishment of self-determination for blacks will have deep effects on the total society. A revolution would not only have to occur *against* white America but *within* white America as well.

The deepest effect on American society would be in the area of policy priorities. The money spent for Vietnam and national defense would have to be reallocated to domestic need. It is impossible to have a policy of "guns and butter." The technical resources—research and development people, engineers, teachers, doctors—do not exist in sufficient numbers to support both a military establishment and institutions of social reform. More basically, the political will does not exist. Congressmen and taxpayers who favor an arms race, a military establishment surpassing that of any country in the world, and a genocidal war in Vietnam, are not capable of understanding or acting on the social needs of the poor in America. It is impossible to maintain a foreign policy of violent counterrevolution but a policy of reform at home. Foreign and domestic policy flow from the same structure of interests. Policy cannot be modified without a movement so massive that it at least threatens those interests; and policy cannot be fundamentally changed without the political defeat of those interests. At a minimum this would mean breaking the power of urban machines and southern congressmen, and placing effective public demands on the major corporations. Without a major change in political leadership, and without the harnessing of business to the achievement of public policy objectives, there can be no meaningful talk of abolishing slums and racism.

Stokely's question is whether whites can give up the benefits they derive from the status quo in order to overturn it. It is certainly true that whites benefit from institutional racism: economic profit, political power, and psychological rewards are derived by various social groups, and the positions of all these groups would be threatened by change. Given this situation, it is inevitable that some whites, in power and out of power, are incapable of learning. But what Stokely's question tends to overlook is the possibility that whites themselves are oppressed by colonialism.

A revolutionary emotion must stem not from personal

shame but from recognition of one's own oppression. Because of American racism, whites are dehumanized and made into beasts. Because of American racism, the society makes "law and order" its paramount objective, preventing social progress —for whites or blacks—in urban development, in education, in medical research, in countless areas of human need. Because of American racism, whites are paying taxes for a government which is less and less able to deal with social problems. And even if America could be imagined without racism, the society would be ridden with problems because of its commitment to the growth of private enterprise and consumption at the expense of social needs. Our cities are unliveable. Our mass media are base. Advertising corrupts the ability for independent thought. Meaningless, hard work is still done by millions of people to support the private luxuries of a few. The technological capacity of this society allows for revolutionary changes in the way men can live, but the American imagination is underdeveloped and poisoned.

When a white American goes beyond shame to a recognition that he is a brain-washed victim of exploitation, then on the basis of self-interest he can begin to work against the colonial status quo. If he is motivated only by personal shame then he will be limited to asking what he can do *for* black people. If he is motivated by personal indignation, however, he will be more able to view black people as possible *allies* in a struggle for change.

The role of whites in the racial crisis can take several forms. First, a white can work inside, or in close relation with, organizations in the black community, particularly as a specialist (lawyer, journalist, fund-raiser, talented organizer). But this is only possible where the white is operating within the approval or discipline of black leadership. Second, the white can work inside the white community directly against racism. This might be educational work (organizing confrontations between ghetto rebels and white church congregations), emergency aid groups to help with fund-raising, legal defense, medical needs in times of crisis, or political protest work (exposure of "respectable" suburbanites who profit from racism as slum-landlords or in other roles). Finally, and most importantly, whites can organize movements which have certain common interests with the black community. These movements can be organized among poor whites (demanding economic changes, such as new housing, which would also benefit blacks), professionals (who want to develop imaginative new roles in the "public sector" free of top-down control), students (who want to reorganize power and purpose in the universities), and the broad cross-section of people who oppose the Vietnam war, the draft, and the growing military budget.

The prospects for such a movement are real. The prospects will grow with the intensification of the racial crisis, and especially with the expansion of the Vietnam war and new Vietnams. The most visible awakening so far is among the students: they are freest of the weight of the past, and temporarily independent of the conservative pressure of family and job. Their growing rebellion in large part has been motivated by the shame of which Stokely speaks—shame at brutality committed by the United States in Mississippi and Vietnam. But their movement is motivated also by an authentic revulsion at their own condition: their sense of being processed and channelled by parents, draft boards, high school and university administrations and the big corporations. Some are coming to the understanding that their passions, imagination, and skills cannot find an outlet in the present context of the society. Their protest movement, as well as the black liberation movement, has triggered a widespread reexamination of purposes throughout the society, particularly among the clergy, intellectuals, and educated professionals.

The important fact about this development is that the protest is occurring in the very heart of the society. The rebellion of black people is understandable because of their political exclusion and economic insecurity. But the revolt in the ranks of the affluent signals a development in some ways more threatening to the powerful. The current men of power cannot count on the younger generation to carry on the tradition of racial arrogance. The unity of the dominating class is breaking down, being challenged from within. Attacked from the outside and divided from within, American colonialism cannot survive. The only issue is how violent its death will be.

The Ghettos, the New Left,
and Some Dangerous Fallacies

Since Mr. Hayden has unqualifiedly called for "abolition of the social work profession," in a paper prepared for the National Conference on Social Welfare, it might well be appropriate for a discussant to respond directly to that particular challenge. But whether or not social work should be abolished is hardly the most important of the issues raised in his presentation. (No doubt it would seem more important to me if I were a social worker.) Surely, the major concern is with the future of Blacks and whites as inhabitants of the United States.

Mr. Hayden has raised so many important issues, that it would take several hours to discuss his presentation fully and with all the care it deserves. Let us deal, primarily, with those matters that he has raised about American society and politics that have the most important implications for the future, not the past, of Black men, women, and children in American ghettos.

There can be no doubt Mr. Hayden is right in saying that the interests of the federal government, and of national coalitions of business, labor, and the churches, do not "coincide with the interests of ghetto dwellers." The "crisis of the cities" is a euphemism that has been repeated with geo-

This chapter is a response to the preceding chapter by Tom Hayden.

metrically increasing frequency and in bolder print each
year since the mid-1950s. First it was the crisis of the men
who owned property in the central business district, who
saw that their investments were rapidly dwindling in value—
and we had urban renewal. Then it was the crisis of the
white suburbanites who had left the city with the help of
HHFA mortgage insurance, and found that driving back into
work was a lengthy and boring daily chore. Moreover they
found that they had no place to dump their automobiles
when they reached downtown. And so we had urban transportation programs and a greater proportion of urban redevelopment projects devoted to downtown parking lots and
garages. Now we have a crisis of the white man's fear, and we
have in response the Urban Coalition, the National Businessmen's Alliance, and the Urban Institute, and great concern
about "crime in the streets."

We have yet to reach the point where our concern is for
the crisis experienced by the Black ghetto dweller, for his
frustration and despair. The "crisis of the cities" has been, and
largely remains, a euphemism for white middle-class financial
risks, esthetic distastes, inconveniences and discomforts, and
fears of physical violence. The motivation for our urban
programs has not been demonstrably a concern for the
problems of the Black man.

But while there is no genuine coincidence of interest between the federal government and the national business, labor,
and church coalitions on the one hand, and the Blacks in the
ghetto, on the other, it may be a bit shortsighted to view with
total disdain the efforts made by the federal government and
national elites. Regardless of the motivations, these are the
only sectors of American society that have made any efforts
to speak of, at all. And they are the only sectors that show
considerable promise in the immediate future. The federal
government and the national coalitions are not more repressive than local governments, merchants, and laborers—not
more reactionary than the great mass of white citizens. They
are at worst in concert with the rest of white society, and
most often out front in seeking to rectify social, economic,
and political injustice. It is the federal government that has

developed and financed Head Start programs, provided voting registrars, ordered public schools desegregated, enacted laws to protect civil rights workers, prohibited segregation in any establishment engaged in interstate commerce.

Such measures, when weighed against several centuries of dehumanization, are relatively minor and mostly token. But it is well to remember that no statutes, court decisions, and domestic Presidential orders of importance are enforceable when they are staunchly opposed. And as Mr. Hayden has pointed out the vast majority of whites in this country are staunchly opposed to gains for Blacks, especially when it means giving up something of their own. In fact the federal government has been far more zealous in enforcing civil rights measures against the wishes of white majorities than it has dared to be in defying majorities on most other issues. If federal efforts for Blacks have been tokens, they have been among the most impressive tokens.

Most of the federal measures on behalf of Blacks (tokens though they may be) have been gained through politics, in most instances, activist pressure politics. The so called "war on poverty" was triggered off as a few writers happened to discover that some of the poor in the United States, in Appalachia, were white. But insistent activist Black political pressure swiftly pulled the focus of the OEO programs to the Black communities. The Supreme Court school desegregation ruling emerged after relentless Black pressures through the judicial process. Since 1948 every democratic presidential candidate has felt a strong need to woo the Black vote, and has taken action to do so.

But Mr. Hayden asserts that Blacks have been far less successful than other groups in their attempts to exercise pressure politics. If by "other groups" he means the tidelands oil men and certain other economic interests he is certainly correct. But if he means white ethnic and religious minorities —the Irish Catholics, the Italian Americans, the Jews—then his assertion is untenable. In point of fact, Black Americans have been far more successful in gaining legislative, judicial, and Presidential concessions for their group than has any white or nonwhite group in this nation's history. In large measure, of course, this can be attributed to the success of these other groups in finding nonpolitical channels of upward mobility. But this does not change the fact that when one considers that (with the possible exception of the Reconstruction Era) Blacks had hardly begun to engage actively in American politics by the end of World War II, the record of accomplishment augurs well for future gains through the political process (in spite of many setbacks that might be cited).

Mr. Hayden's assertion that "pressure politics," as he terms it, is not a possible avenue through which Black Americans can bring about meaningful change becomes all the more curious as he contradicts his own position when he makes his most specific recommendations for actions to be undertaken by Blacks. For these specific recommendations are, after all, for Blacks to engage in "pressure politics." He calls for "united political organizations of a coalition character" to teach people organizing skills—to organize tenants, welfare mothers, youth groups, educational workshops, or electoral campaigns to build up voting power for bargaining purposes to break the power of urban machines. This seems highly sensible, especially as a complementary effort for trying to get the federal resources that have already been allocated, used more effectively, more justly, and more humanely in the ghetto. It can also, of course, be a means for accelerating the flow of local dollars and the federal dollars as local authorities under pressure squeeze Washington for help. In spite of his sweeping condemnation of the American political process as a fruitless arena of activity for Blacks, Mr. Hayden's specific suggestions are for actions and measures that can well be, and in fact, are being accomplished within that framework.

But his sweeping characterizations do not always end up so happily. His facile characterization of America as a colonial society blinds him to the ultimate nightmare that will likely ensue if his visions of rebellion become a reality. In spite of the fact that he continually calls attention to the highly repressive racist tendencies of the white majority in America he comforts himself with the assurance that the practical risks of exercising repression would moderate white response to open violence and to nationwide attacks designed to bring about social crisis and anarchy. But all signs read otherwise. One has only to reread Mr. Hayden's paper to find one compelling indication after another that violence and anarchy will be met with repression.

And it is here that Mr. Hayden's characterization of America as a colonial society has let him down. For the analogy misfires on a key point, and it is not one of the three objections he has dealt with. Certainly white Americans have exploited Black Americans, and certainly America is not a melting pot. But the exploiters are not a minority and in strange land far from their own shores. They are not the British in India, the Dutch in Southeast Asia, the French in Africa. White Americans are an overwhelming and powerful majority in their own land. In the face of Black rebellion and revolution white Americans will not retreat to a distant homeland from which they once set sail to build a far-flung empire. Long before the point where retreat is indicated the reaction will set in. And I fear that Mr. Hayden fails to see the full potentialities of that nightmare. The worst he sees is that the revolutionary might go to jail. But there are far worse eventualities than that. Unfortunately there are some contemporary models—in South Africa, for example, but perhaps even worse are our own Indian reservations or some of our historical plantation models. Mr. Hayden doesn't feel that white Americans would cordon off the central cities, never to return to them, because of the economic losses involved. But Ray Vernon and many other economists who have been examining the trends and patterns in our economy have come to the conclusion that there is little reason any longer for commerce and industry to be geographically centralized at all, let alone in the central city.

I stress this pessimistic view of repressive extremes not only because I feel they are possible responses to open rebellion and anarchy, but also because I feel that we must see beyond "going to jail" as a likely ultimate penalty for rebellion. Going to jail may be the ultimate penalty for a white middle class radical protester, but hardly for a lower class black man.

If we see this, we may be forced, perhaps frightened, into thinking and acting in a frame of reference that makes the urgent need for constructive change all the more apparent and all the sooner fulfilled.

Mr. Hayden makes some excellent constructive suggestions in his paper for both Blacks and whites. And he makes a particularly telling point that anticipates my comments about the latent repressiveness of white America. He says "those who fear repression tend to lecture militants when they should be proving with deeds that meaningful change can be accomplished within the present framework of society." In this statement Mr. Hayden issues a particularly salient challenge to the social work profession. He has called for the profession's abolition because, in his view, it functions as part of the repressive machinery of American society. Certainly it is not in the vanguard of revolution. The National Association of Social Workers finally got around to holding a Vietnam and Poverty Protest when Huburt Humphrey announced his candidacy for the Presidency. But by that time, the phenomenon was so stale that the *Washington Post* and the *New York Times* did not even regard the event as newsworthy.

One option for social work is to undertake the specific actions suggested by Mr. Hayden, both among Blacks and whites. The only problem is that for most social workers this would probably mean that their salaries would be cut off, and they would have to live from hand to mouth until their work has been effective enough to draw some support from the larger society. I don't believe social work will be abolished (even if it should be) but it will probably die unless the younger members are willing to take the chances necessary in order to truly work with and on behalf of the repressed Blacks. There is little chance that the older members will. The profession may already be dead. It certainly seems that social work has been a comparatively meaningless activity in the 1960s.

WHITNEY M. YOUNG, JR.

Planning, Politics, and Social Change

In light of recent events, it can be said that our nation is closer to catastrophe than it has ever been. In the words of John F. Kennedy, "if peaceful evolution is not possible, then violent revolution is inevitable."

The brutal assassination of Dr. Martin Luther King, Jr., in Memphis, the riots that were the direct result of it, the urgent warnings of the President's Commission on Civil Disorders on the meaning and extent of white racism, the dramatic upheavals on the nation's college campuses, increasing black militancy, the failure of the Congress to act on the just demands of the poor and the increasing polarization of the races all provide fearsome promise of further tragedy unless America can be turned around, unless America can, at long last, find the heart to act with that compassion and understanding for our common humanity that alone can produce solutions to the problems that threaten us with domestic chaos.

The question today is not whether we are, or are not, in for social change. Social change is inevitable. The question is whether it will be for good or for ill, and unless present trends are aborted we are very likely to alter for the worse much of what is most valuable in our society.

If, when the tears for Martin Luther King are dried, the Congress has responded with no more than the enactment of a Civil Rights Bill—which the record indicates had little, or no, chance of adoption until the assassin struck—while leaving questions of housing and employment, schooling, social pathology, and a massive national commitment aside, we will have failed as a nation and Martin Luther King will have died in vain.

The Report of the Riot Commission stands incontrovertibly as a moral indictment of the nation. It delineates our movement toward two societies, one white, one black—separate and unequal. It exposes white racism—the refusal of white Americans to accept Negroes as human beings, as social and economic equals—in all its present and historic virulence. It is like a fiscal audit that says we are bankrupt, or a medical audit that says we are in the grips of a terminal disease. As a nation, we can ignore it only at national peril.

The Report places responsibility for the creation of the black ghetto on white institutions. "White institutions created it, white institutions maintain it and white society condones it. . . ." This is the Commission's major finding, the finding of white racism.

The Report goes on to say that "this nation will deserve neither safety nor progress until it can demonstrate the wisdom and the will to undertake decisive action against the root causes of racial disorder."

In large measure, this country's future, its success or failure, will be determined by the success or failure of Negro Americans in their struggle for existence in the urban environment, and by the success or failure of white Americans in redeeming the circumstances under which the bulk of American Negroes live. The real test of the urban structure will be whether or not the Negro within it benefits and succeeds on a par with his white peers.

I make no apology for concentrating on the plight of the Negro poor. If we can redeem the ghettos and solve the problems of the Negro poor, we will have solved the problems for all of America's poor.

It is unfortunate that it took riots to bring the facts of ghetto life to the attention of most people, and that it took the Report of the President's Riot Commission to bring us face to face with the nature of white racism.

The issue, however, is no longer whether we can find solutions but whether we *will*. As President Johnson said in his State of the Union message in January 1968, "any nation that can send a man to the moon, can put every man in a house." This is the perspective in which we must proceed. Our technology, our social philosophy and our national resources, perhaps for the first time in the history of man, make it possible to do almost anything we set out to do. The crisis we face is still one of manageable proportions. Solutions are not beyond our powers of invention. But we are in a race against time.

Some Needed Steps

As a beginning, we need to do massively what, to date, we have only done experimentally. By this I mean that we need to review the vast history of poverty-related programs conducted throughout the nation to determine which have proved successful and then apply our successes across the board on a scale designed to affect the lives of people by the hundreds and thousands and tens of thousands, rather than by the tens and twenties.

The Urban League recently compiled a study of 815 federally financed antipoverty programs in seventy-nine cities, programs in which it had participated or with which it was familiar. Collectively they covered the waterfront, ranging from Head Start to Adult Basic Education, and from the Neighborhood Youth Corps to Manpower and Small Business Development. We found that 76 per cent had shown good-to-excellent results, yet where is the massive application which alone can effect the lives of the bulk of the poor? The sad fact is that most demonstration projects die unnoticed.

Add to the federally financed antipoverty programs all of those that have been generated in the private sector by foundations, social welfare agencies, university research centers, and by business and industry and the total volume of successful experiments is staggering.

We need to build on our successes without further delay. The time is past for halfway measures, token gestures, and small-scale, one-dimensional efforts, no matter how well intentioned. If we are to resolve the urban–racial crisis while it is still of manageable proportions, we must act now or face the danger of its rapidly becoming one of unmanageable proportions.

We need to make optimum use of all the most advanced techniques for data-gathering and analysis. Systems engineering and operations research, applied to the problems of the ghetto, hold the promise of greatly clarifying complex urban interrelationships.

Historically, our cities have grown by random accretion, the result of hundreds of thousands of individual decisions by private builders and public agencies, largely unrelated to one another except by accident. Nearly all the measures so far taken to repair the damage, from traditional city planning to urban renewal, have tended to follow on a somewhat bigger scale the same random, uncoordinated, piecemeal approach that generated many of our problems in the first place.

Systems engineering at its most ambitious would, by contrast, examine the city in its totality, interrelating all its demographic, economic, social, and physical components, and produce coordinated approaches to the maze of interlocking problems that confound us.

We are sorely in need of an over-all system of social accounting, calculated to pinpoint our social well-being or lack of it. Just as we once floundered in the area of economic policy for the lack of hard, factual information, so today we are floundering in the area of adequate social policy due to the lack of hard, factual information.

At present, data affecting the urban–racial crisis is scattered all over the landscape, but it is rarely put together in a readable fashion and never, except on the most limited terms, on a national basis. As one acute observer has pointed out, "the lack of regular information fosters an innocence and irresponsibility that is positively terrifying."

City after city launches urban renewal projects, for instance, only to discover, with horror, that poor people are being dislocated from their homes. State after state pushes gigantic highway projects only to discover, with astonishment, that enclaves of poor are often effectively cut off and isolated from the rest of the community.

The National Commission on Technology, Automation and Economic Progress, on which I had the honor of serving, unanimously reported that our ability to measure social progress was far behind our capacity to measure economic change. We found that we had far "too few yardsticks to tell us how we are doing," and recommended that "a system of social accounts" be established to provide systematic information on the nation's social health and on its needs, and to provide the basis for policy decisions in all areas of social welfare.

In the twenty-odd years since the establishment of the Council of Economic Advisors, we have developed a very sophisticated capacity to register every vibration in the U.S. economy. The Economic Report today is a good example of the staggering number of things Americans do that are regularly reported and tabulated. At a minimum, the statistics act as warning signals. When things are not going well, when growth slows or unemployment rises, people know about it and corrective action is taken. Almost the exact opposite prevails in the social field.

Adoption of a system of social accounting would lead to the development of similarly usable indicators for taking the nation's social pulse and devising programs based on the most stable insights into our national realities.

When testimony to starvation and near-starvation in Mississippi began to emerge before congressional committees a year or more ago, it was incredible to find that high-ranking public officials had to admit, shamefacedly, their ignorance of the situation. Nobody, it turned out, knew the extent or degree or geographical distribution of hunger and malnutrition in America.

The Secretary of Agriculture, who runs the food programs, did not know. The Surgeon General of the United States did not know. The Director of the Office of Economic Opportunity did not know. The Secretary of Health, Education and Welfare did not know.

It is entirely possible that if we had then had a reliable set of social indicators established, such suffering could never have come to pass. The warning signals would have been recognized and a humane society would have acted to correct what it cannot tolerate.

All our social planning aimed at the urban–racial crisis should take place within the framework of a Domestic Marshall Plan, a term signifying the necessary level of national commitment to progress toward domestic peace and urban tranquility. The Urban League has long advocated such an approach, one commensurate with the magnitude of the problems we face. Surely this country, with its unparalleled affluence, can do for its poor and for its threatened cities what it did so generously for our former allies—and our former enemies—after World War II.

A Domestic Marshall Plan should be tied to a timetable calculated to produce visible evidence of progress on a year by year basis. We've set timetables in the space race and in the building of supersonic planes and we've met them. Residents of the ghetto are not unrealistic—if anything, they are supremely realistic—and they know that results cannot be produced overnight. What they do require, however, is visible evidence that the white community cares, that action is at long last launched which within a reasonable span of time will produce real results and permit incorporation of the Negro minority into the mainstream of American life.

Within the broad outlines of a Domestic Marshall Plan, we need to set priorities and establish a sequence of first steps designed for maximum initial results. Given the ghetto Negro's need for a "top dollar" job and the unchallenged necessity to rebuild the nation's black ghettos, the Urban League advocates the immediate appropriation of 10 billion dollars for the emergency implementation of existing federal housing laws. Such a step, an essential *first* step, has the virtues of simplicity and the power to effect major changes in the ghettos within a relatively short period of time. Its ramifications for creating "top dollar" jobs for Negroes in the construction industry are on a par with its ramifications for creating a new and improved housing stock within the ghetto.

The Department of Housing and Urban Development has

the basic housing tools at hand, including tools which place construction and management in the hands of competitive private enterprise. The bottleneck in production now is the current meager level of appropriations.

Spending 10 billion dollars for new construction would require the recruitment of thousands and thousands of new workers who should come from the ghetto. To draw on the ghetto denies nothing to white workers already employed in the construction trades. It is only new jobs, derived from a massive increase in the rate of construction, that would go to Negroes.

Given the ghetto Negro's low educational achievement, there is only one kind of "top dollar" job he can get—construction work—and if the gap between whites and Negroes is to be closed, the Negro has to have a "top dollar" job. White school dropouts have been doing construction work for centuries and getting well paid for it in the process. There is no reason why we shouldn't utilize an emergency construction program to crack open the cycle of poverty.

Such a move would provide evidence of a national commitment to real and substantial action. Any failure to make such a commitment now is simply an invitation to more of the kind of "instant urban renewal" that occurred in Detroit and Newark and in Washington, D.C., and Chicago.

We've taken stronger action than this in behalf of all sorts of other groups. Take the farmers, for instance. White immigrants were given free land to farm, and then they were given low interest loans to enable them to buy farm machinery. Then the Department of Agriculture sent out farm agents to show them how to use their machines and how to rotate their crops. These were all free services. Now we pay farmers not to produce in order to maintain farm prices.

The process of subsidy, direct and indirect, reaches almost everywhere but to the poor. If we subsidize middle class homeowners, expanding businesses, farmers who are paid not to grow crops, and ships carrying foreign trade, why can't we also subsidize the poor in the form of jobs to create housing?

While the motivation for, and the implementation of, massive national action aimed at the ghettos must come from all significant quarters in our society, it is clear that the general outlines for national action will be established through political channels at the local, state, and national levels. It is equally clear that the social work profession has an obligation, beyond any it has yet discharged, to influence the course of political developments in the area of social welfare.

Operating social welfare programs provide the most sensitive possible instrument for spotting emergent needs and problems in urban areas and for identifying weak spots in the social fabric. No other profession is more sensitively attuned to, or more daily aware of, the problems requiring resolution or the factors contributing to social dysfunction. In terms of the urban–racial crisis, no other profession is closer to the subject, more aware of the end results of inadequate social policy, or more sensitively equipped to advise the body politic. Yet it took members of the President's Riot Commission, who were rank novices in the ghetto, observing what social workers have observed at intimate range for years, to detail and delineate the picture effectively for public consumption.

I am inclined to think of the social work profession as a sleeping giant, unaware of its own powers. The social work profession has had a measurable influence in the development of social policy, but all too frequently its influence has had to be measured in millimeters rather than miles. I seriously question whether we have ever fully utilized the muscle inherent in the social work structure.

It is common enough for individual social work agencies to take top-level policy positions with respect to given issues, on specific pieces of legislation and on public proposals. And it is common enough to find such positions embodied in resolution form and forwarded by mail to the appropriate authorities—usually, however, with limited effect. It is rare, if not unknown, for social work agencies, singly or collectively, to mount consistent, hard-hitting, wide-ranging campaigns, year in and year out, in behalf of desirable public policy.

While there was no lack of unanimity among us, for example, on the 1967 amendments to the Social Security Act, one clear measure of our all-too-frequent impotence was the minimal impact we had on the final outcome. Nor have we registered any notable successes when faced with threatened reductions in essential domestic programs like rent supplements, Model Cities. and antipoverty programs, in and out of the OEO. All too frequently, we see desirable legislation established on the books and then stand helplessly by while it founders for lack of appropriations or while appropriations are cut back in some ill-conceived fashion. Despite our commitment to the poor we have learned little about the art of advocacy or the effective use of political power.

Previous papers have dealt at length with the complexities of the decision-making process in the public arena, but the simple fact remains that the political establishment is open to influence—attack, if need be—at every step, level, and juncture.

A unified position on the part of every major social welfare agency or organization in any major metropolitan area, aggressively pursued from the local to the federal level, would have an impact of impressive proportions; the more so were such an effort to be mounted on a national basis.

The AMA and the American Bar Association have influence far beyond their specific numbers and I see no reason, since we are not seriously divided in our objectives or on the details of a social work agenda for the future, why the social work profession cannot proceed, with equal skill, to affect the establishment of public policy.

Equally important, and generally overlooked, is our capacity to generate action on the part of our client-constituency and our failure to mobilize and utilize the collective power and political potential inherent in agency boards.

Each of us has a clientele, a constituency which can be organized into an effective political instrument, versed in the issues which affect its welfare and vocal in pursuit of them. We have a leadership role to exercise among the poor which few social welfare agencies have taken the pains to develop. The point is not to speak *for* the poor, but to generate a strong community voice for removal of the legal and social barriers to their advancement and upward mobility. The local citizenry at the grassroots can be a powerful political force if it has some assistance in mobilizing and organizing its latent strengths.

The collective membership on agency boards in any one community is a force of great magnitude, one which generally represents the entire spectrum of the local establishment, but which too often goes unexploited and unutilized as a political force. It should be borne in mind that every member of your board has a social constituency of his own which can be mobilized in support of your objectives. Board members, after all, are not selected for their lack of ties within the community and those ties should be fully explored and enlisted in the struggle.

In most communities, a coalition of social work agencies is well within reason. We should seek out all possible ways to act in concert. Coalition politics can take many forms ranging from *ad hoc* coalitions mobilized around a specific issue to continuing coalitions organized around a full spectrum of issues. Since our areas of agreement are far broader than our areas of disagreement, we have nothing to lose and everything to gain by utilizing our combined forces for effective action.

The important thing in coalition politics is how to get critical concessions—the concessions that count. Given essential agreement on our values and objectives, the best strategies are the purely pragmatic ones, the ones that work. Sometimes it takes 50,000 people mobilized behind a given idea and sometimes it only takes the right man in the right place at the right time. Indeed, there are times when a threat of action may be more powerful than the action itself—and even a great deal more preferable. We are in a war and a war calls for a whole array of tactics and strategies, from direct confrontation to conciliation and, under reasonable circumstances, compromise.

There is an overriding need to guard against an overly cautious approach. Too often, because of our intimate acquaintance with the nuances of the *status quo*, we set objectives which are only marginally meaningful. We must be far more aggressive. We should always first consider what the most far-reaching goal would be, with the widest impact on the system. The "revolutionary solution" ought to be examined first. Good planning proceeds backward, rejecting the totally unrealistic until arriving at a policy which is within the realm of the attainable. Too often our program goals fall short of social changes which events prove were really within reach.

Furthermore, there is no reason why social workers shouldn't take an active part in local politics at the grassroots level. Social workers usually have no choice in the selection of candidates because they just don't get involved. Tax exemptions impose some limitations, but social workers tend to respond to the tax exemption with more sensitivity and conservatism than other groups similarly affected and overlook the wide latitude for action they do have.

White social workers have a prime responsibility to exercise leadership in the white community to do away with white racism. It isn't enough just to work in the ghetto with the disadvantaged or fall in line behind Negro leadership. It's important to stand as witnesses in the white community, in those areas of prime resistance—in John Birch territory; in communities like Cicero, Ilinois; in George Wallace territory.

In short, the latent strength within the social work profession must be aroused and utilized. The sleeping giant must be awakened. We are in a position to command electrifying change and the times demand that we exercise our full strength. No other group is more sensitively located in relation to the problems. There is no excuse for timorousness. Events loudly demand that we examine our organizational direction and machinery with a view to making whatever adjustments are necessary to maximize our potential for greater impact. We must operate with optimum effectiveness, drawing on all our resources, if we are to meet the challenge of America's most pressing unfinished business. To fail to do so is to fail our constituencies, our obligations, our nation, and ourselves.

If the business community can marshall its resources, as it is doing, for a concerted onslaught on the problems of the ghetto, the social work profession, which has an historic commitment to social solutions, can do no less.

If there was anything heartening to be learned from recent ghetto riots, it was the sudden, if belated, awakening of business and industry to their social responsibilities in the ghetto and to the ghetto poor.

In the wake of the 1967 Newark riots, Orville Beal, president of Prudential Insurance, which has its national headquarters in Newark, said, "We as businessmen have no one to blame but ourselves for what happened last summer." Stanley Marcus, of Neiman-Marcus in Dallas, sent a letter to all his manufacturers and suppliers requiring that they pursue a policy of equal opportunity employment. "In the future," he said, "we would rather do business with a company which is actively and sincerely pursuing a policy of equal opportunity, than to continue to do business with one which is not . . . (a matter that) will be considered by all our buyers."

This is the kind of vigorous thinking that has informed and inspired the business community, that led to the creation of the Urban Coalition, and more recently the National Businessmen's Alliance. This is the kind of thinking that inspired the U.S. Chamber of Commerce and the National Association of Manufacturers to take action. If such traditionally conservative and traditionally detached elements in the community can respond with clarity and insight, recognizing the full range of their stake in the social health of the cities, surely the social work profession can marshall its energies and exercise leadership within the full range of its resources.

Nor can we disregard the challenge from the young. One of the most significant current developments is the determination and the mood of young people, both white and black, who view adult values and practices with, at best, cynicism and, at worst, contempt. They are aware of and repulsed by the hypocrisies of adult society and the gap between American philosophy and practice. Today's young people are challenging the tenets of this society and we can't write off that challenge.

The hour is late. We are in a race against time to end the poverty and bigotry which distort our national life. Whether we build a new, democratic society together, whether we end in an orgy of violence or in a slow, painful process of decay, depends upon the decisions we make today and the resources we marshall to implement them.

There are, in reality, only three alternatives.

The first is genocide. It has been used in the past by nations determined to rid themselves of a minority they would not live with, the model for which has been set by Adolf Hitler.

The second is apartheid: a means to ending the present hyprocrisy of the present caste system by formalizing it. Our model here is Verwoerd's South Africa. There is far more of South Africa in our society than many Americans are, even yet, prepared to believe.

The third way is the path of reason and responsibility, and this is the course we must surely follow. It means closing the gap which separates our two nations, ending racism, and giving Negroes an equal share in both the rewards and the responsibilities of citizenship. Our models here are the American Constitution and the Judeo-Christian ethic. Only in this way can justice be served and democracy survive. "All that is necessary for the triumph of evil is that good men do nothing."

Index

DATE DUE